The General Said
"Nuts"

Firsthand Accounts
of Wartime Heroism,
Horror,
and Humor

The General Said "Nuts"

Firsthand Accounts of Wartime Heroism, Horror, and Humor

By Bill Walraven

Edited by Marjorie Walraven

Javelina Press
Corpus Christi, Texas

© 2009 Javelina Press
Corpus Christi, Texas

All rights reserved

ISBN 978-0-9646325-7-8

Library of Congress Control Number: 2009913011

Columns reprinted by permission of Stephen W. Sullivan
Publisher and President
Corpus Christi Caller-Times
October 13, 1989

By the author:
    History:
        Corpus Christi: History of a Texas Seaport
        El Rincon: A History of Corpus Christi Beach
    With Marjorie Walraven:
        The Magnificent Barbarians: Little-told Tales of the Texas Revolution
        Gift of the Wind: The Corpus Christi Bayfront
        Empresarios' Children: The Welders of Texas
        Wooden Rigs-Iron Men: The Story of Oil and Gas in South Texas

    Humor:
        Real Texans Don't Drink Scotch in Their Dr Pepper
        Walraven's World or Star Boarder (and Other) Wars
        All I Know Is What's on TV: What Will Rogers Would Say Today

Cover medals (from top):
    Distinguished Service Cross
    Navy Cross
    Distinguished Flying Cross

In 1947 in *Tales of the South Pacific* James Michener wrote of the warriors of World War II:

". . . longer and longer shadows will obscure [them] until their Guadalcanal sounds distant on the ear like Shiloh and Valley Forge."

Now the years have passed. Michener's words have come true, and other names—like Heartbreak Ridge and the Chosin Reservoir, Hue and Hamburger Hill, Baghdad, Anwar, and Kandahar Province—have joined the annals of American heroism. Younger generations have little or no knowledge of Iwo Jima, Bataan, or the Battle of the Bulge, where U.S. Army Gen. Anthony McAuliffe uttered one word in circumstances that ironically illustrate the indomitable spirit of the American military.

Photo by Wilson Walraven

This quotation at the World War II Memorial on the Mall in Washington, D.C., expresses the appreciation of a grateful nation.

'Nuts'

In the heat of wartime battle there are many sayings made that ring forever in military history:

"Don't give up the ship!"
"Don't fire until you see the whites of their eyes!"
"Damn the torpedoes! Full speed ahead!"
"You may fire when ready, Gridley!"
And "Nuts!"

The latter was uttered by Brigadier Gen. Anthony C. McAuliffe in response to a German demand that the 101st Airborne Division, surrounded at a Belgian crossroads named Bastogne, surrender.

The battle started on December 16, 1944, when twenty-eight German divisions unexpectedly drove through the Ardennes Forest under heavy ground cloud cover in the last great offensive the Germans were able to muster in World War II. No one had seen the German buildup, and the American Army was taken by surprise.

Warren Watson, who was a young lieutenant in the 101st, says the 28th Division bore the brunt of the attack, having been placed in a relatively quiet area to recuperate after bloody fighting.

"They took a beating. We were ordered to move up, but the entire Corps, which had been using Bastogne as headquarters, was in retreat—tanks, trucks, everything. There was one two-lane road and they were using both lanes. We were finally able to turn through them and get to an open field. The 501st Parachute Regiment was sent ahead to engage the enemy. They really got into it. Then the 502nd and 506th regiments went in. And with the 327th we held a circle five miles in diameter."

They were finding out how much firepower the Germans had concentrated. The Germans intended to capture Antwerp, a major Allied supply center. This was the beginning of a desperate battle in which the 101st would be battered by artillery.

"At one point I was liaison between regiment and division, attending general conferences and taking information back to the colonels. We were staying in a long narrow room. An artillery shell came through several floors and exploded in the room I had just left, killing everyone in it.

"Things were getting desperate. After two weeks the men were exhausted. We were almost out of ammunition. The only food left was K rations, and that was getting low. The weather grounded our planes. There were several armored Panzer divisions outside the circle. They went around but never came through. They could have walked over us."

The men expected a major assault at any time. Then three German officers came through the line under a white flag to F Company. They asked to speak to the commanding officer.

"Gen. Maxwell Taylor, our commanding general, had been called back to Washington for a conference," Watson said. "General McAuliffe, an artillery officer, was the ranking general. The Germans gave him a note giving us two hours to surrender. I was standing beside McAuliffe when he looked at the paper. He acted like he didn't know what to do. He said, 'Oh, nuts.' He said it as you might say, 'Oh, my goodness.'

"A German asked the other what he had said. He repeated, 'Nuts.' They were belligerent. They just stomped off. I thought I would find the deepest hole around because the world was about to fall on us.

"Strangely enough, nothing happened. A German fighter plane dropped a bomb and blew up the roof of the building I was in. That's when I was wounded. The next day the sun came out, and our planes went on the attack. Patton broke through and I was hauled out. But the 101st didn't get any rest. Patton made them lead in breaking out and the Germans were dug in."

History is written in cold type, without emotion or voice inflection. And "Nuts!" was heard around the world, not as a perplexed exclamation but as a chin-jutting expletive of defiance.

(December 16, 1988)

[Headquarters, Third U.S. Army, General Orders No. 14 (January 14, 1945):

The President of the United States takes pleasure in presenting the Distinguished Service Cross to Anthony Clement McAuliffe (0-12263), Brigadier General, U.S. Army, for extraordinary heroism in connection with military operations against an armed enemy while serving as Acting Commander, 101st Airborne Division, in action against enemy forces from 17 to 26 December 1944, at Bastogne, Belgium.

. . .

Brigadier General McAuliffe's courage, fearless determination and inspiring, heroic leadership exemplify the highest traditions of the military forces of the United States and reflect great credit upon himself, the 101st Airborne Division, and the United States Army.]

The legions of fighting men of the Great War of 1914–1918 are gone, and the ranks of those who served in World War II, like McAuliffe and others of the brave 101st, are thinning every day.

This book is a compilation of their experiences—most of them first-hand accounts, a few from World War I doughboys and their contemporaries but most from veterans of World War II.

Along with the stories of heroism and horror, the author adds stories of his personal experiences, most of them in a different kind of war—the war of men who served in lonely outposts, far from home and also far from the glory and excitement of combat. His stories, most told with humor, provide a counterpoint that serves to emphasize the courage and dedication of the American spirit.

Contents

'Nuts' 7

Before the Great War 17

The War To End All Wars 23

Pearl Harbor 38

Dark Days 53

No Peace in the Pacific 69

To D-Day and Beyond 103

The Wild Blue Yonder 133

The Final Days 147

A Different Kind of War 153

Resolution 219

Illustrations

World War II Memorial on the Washington Mall	6
The Memorial Cemetery of the Pacific	15
U.S. Army Cavalry soldier on horseback	17
Biplane	23
Japanese pilot's view of Battleship Row on December 7, 1941	38
Japanese pilot's view of damage	53
Pearl Harbor's Bowfin Park Waterfront Memorial to submarines and their crews lost in World War II	69
The USS *Borie* as it entered the Port of Corpus Christi in 1926	103
Crew of B-24 immediately after return from mission	133
The *Enola Gay* on Tinian	147
PT 259 and crew on Midway Island	153
U.S. sailors giving Military Honors to Japanese pilots killed in the Battle of Midway	219

Preface

I was visiting an old cousin in Georgia some years back, and she asked what I did for a living.

I said, "I go out and talk to people. Then I go back and write it up for the newspaper."

She thought for a moment and then said, " 'Pears to me you've got a job with all the work squeezed out of it."

I had to agree with her. It wasn't like work. It was fun. It was satisfying.

Sometimes you have to pry a story out, but usually people are flattered to find someone interested in them and to be asked to tell about their life. When you deal with people, you never run out of stories. This was particularly true of the men who fought in our biggest war.

While many were so modest it was hard to get them to talk, most were glad to be recognized for their part in it. They told funny stories, gut-wrenching stories, and some that offered information never before revealed.

One gave the startling twist to the answer Gen. McAuliffe gave to the Germans at Bastogne. Another told the true story of the bridge over the River Kwai. Others recalled the heroism, horrors, suffering, and boredom in various services around the world. Many recalled humorous incidents. These are among some 3,500 articles I collected during fifteen years of column writing.

On a far less heroic note were my own experiences on a PT Boat in the Pacific. Most read more like the script from the television comedy "McHale's Navy" than a heroic epic. Our main enemy was boredom.

Like so many other sailors, soldiers, Marines, and Coast Guardsmen, other PT squadrons fought heroic battles and suffered terrible losses.

I salute them all.

Bill Walraven

Memorial Day

Photo by the author

The National Memorial Cemetry of the Pacific, also known as the Punchbowl National Cemetry in Honolulu, Hawaii, is a memorial to men and women who served in the United States armed forces.

We tend to forget what holidays were originally for. Today Memorial Day is mainly for going to the beach, barbecuing on the patio, watching an automobile race on the tube, or making an indentation in the couch. Sometimes it's good to remember why we are getting this time for relaxation.

Memorial Day should be time for a few memories. Among mine is a red-headed, freckled-faced kid who smiled a lot but never had much to say. He still had his hair cut short as a reminder of Navy boot camp when a torpedo sank his destroyer off the coast of Alaska, drowning him and all his shipmates in the frigid waters.

That was early in World War II, and his death was my first hint that war was not a great, fun adventure. I remember a boy who was my best friend and a good Marine. In the steaming jungle of

Guadalcanal, he was felled by a rare fever, the cure of it beyond the knowledge of doctors. He wasted away and died and is buried far from home.

The day was originally called Decoration Day because some Southern ladies started decorating the graves of both Union and Confederate soldiers on May 30 during the War Between the States. The same observance in the North was known as Memorial Day, which now serves the entire country. The idea was believed to have been that of Cassandra Oliver Moncure, a Virginia woman of French origin. May 30 was the French Memorial Day, "The Day of Ashes," which commemorated the return of Napoleon Bonaparte's remains from St. Helena to France.

Memorial Day is a time for remembering those who died in all wars. So I remember finding the graves of two young Georgia soldiers—my grandfather's brothers. One lies in a lonely grave in a motte in a pasture in eastern Tennessee. The other is in the Confederate Cemetery in Richmond, Virginia.

I remember a big, red-faced boy, older than I, who once taught me table manners in the orphanage where I grew up. He died a Marine hero, charging a Japanese pillbox on some all-but-forgotten island in the South Pacific. I remember a college classmate who had something of a drinking problem as he made an unsuccessful transition from World War II combat soldier to college student. Alcohol made him wild, and he was in several scrapes before he re-enlisted in the Army to avoid punishment. The day before hostilities ended in Korea, he stepped from his foxhole and an enemy shell landed beside him, killing him instantly.

There was a local high school graduate who told his friends at his going-away party that he knew with certainty he wasn't coming back. His premonition was correct. He died with a North Vietnamese bullet through the head. There are others who stir in our memories with less and less frequency as the years go by. All have one thing in common. They will never grow old.

In Arlington and other national cemeteries we have memorials to heroes who died for the rest of us. In Corpus Christi's Old Bayview Cemetery lie victims of the Mexican War and the Civil War. In various other places are those from World War I, World War II, Korea, and Vietnam.

Markings on the early ones grow faint. Memorials are almost forgotten. So on Memorial Day, between trips to the refrigerator, take time to remember those for whom the day is meant.

(May 29, 1989)

Before the Great War

A later-day U.S cavalry soldier, like those who fought against Pancho Villa in the early days of the twentieth century

A lot of old Navy hands think they are pretty salty, but few are older or saltier than R. L. "Bob" McComb.

"Teddy Roosevelt thought there was too much drinking and low living in the Navy," McComb said. "He ordered 1,300 fifteen-year-olds recruited to improve the quality of the Navy. I was one of those fifteen-year-olds in 1901. I served aboard the square-rigged sailing vessel *Mojakin*, until I passed my exams to second-class seaman. Then I served on the destroyer *Paul Jones*.

"We sailed up and down the West Coast and went to Panama nine months before they opened the canal. My opinion is that Uncle Sam was foolish to turn the canal loose after all the suffering those soldiers went through to clear that place out.

"We lost a lot of soldiers there, but you don't hear about that anymore. We backed up 300 feet from the wharf because of the huge tides. We had all guns trimmed on Colombia. Panama was trying to get independence from Colombia. Both Atlantic and Pacific fleets were there. I'm sure we told Columbia if they didn't give Panama its freedom, we'd blow them off the map.

"The Navy was rough in those days. Stokers shoveling coal in the boiler rooms had it particularly bad in the tropics. They were black when they came out of that hole. Poor devils.

"The first thing I had to do was learn to fight. I took boxing lessons and fought. I had to quit because my hands got busted up. All you had to do was to go to certain joints ashore and if you wanted a fight, you were welcome."

A young man had to fight to survive. Officers were pretty rough on enlisted men, too.

"We almost had to get down on our knees to them," he said. "If you got in trouble, they put you in leg or arm irons and fed you bread and water."

When McComb was discharged in 1907 at age twenty-one, he was offered a contract to play professional baseball with the Seattle team. "I played in the field and pitched for them for two years while I was in the Navy. They offered me $125 a month and expenses. But my mother said I had been away from home long enough. I was a third class gunner's mate when I left. If I had re-enlisted, I would have been promoted to second class.

"I came home and went to work in Uehlinger's bakery for $27 a month. But I did play for the Corpus Christi baseball team with Matt Pelligrino, Claud Shannon, Ed Gollihar, and all those fellows.

"When World War I came around, I didn't go. I was with the Post Office then, and it was already depleted by the draft. I didn't really mind. I'd had enough of the sea by then."

(January 16, 1979)

'We were loyal to Roosevelt. We would have died for him.'

In the earliest days of the twentieth century, before the two great world wars, American fighting men were already engaged in foreign operations. One of them was Jackson E. Baker, who was 102 in September 1980. Baker had a lot of stories.

He was, he said, "born in 1878, went with Teddy Roosevelt to San Juan Hill in the Spanish-American War, played professional baseball under Connie Mack with the Philadelphia Athletics in 1908-10, was on the first American destroyer sunk in World War I, was a contractor for years" and still enjoyed an active love life.

He didn't much want to talk about the Spanish-American War "because a feller is doing a book on me." He did say his cavalry unit was backing up Teddy and was preparing to charge when Roosevelt carried the day.

"We were loyal to Roosevelt. We would have died for him. He was a man you couldn't help but like, and he was the only Republican I have ever voted for. I saw him when he came through West Texas as president. And once I saluted Harry Truman when he was taking a walk in Independence, Missouri. He saluted back and shook hands. I think he and Teddy Roosevelt were our two greatest presidents."

He got out of baseball because it didn't pay much. "Top pay," he said, "was $500 a month. I didn't get that much." He described Connie Mack, the A's manager, as "a good old Irishman, if you produced."

He was aboard the USS *Jacob Jones* when it was sunk by a German sub in World War I. An English ship picked up most of the crewmen.

"I don't feel the government owes me a thing," he said. "I owe the government for freedom."

Another early day veteran was Bob Essing, who came to the Southwest as a member of the Maryland National Guard when Pancho Villa started acting up before the United States entered World War I. The American Army chased Villa as far as Monterrey.

"But he was always on the other side of the mountain," Essing said. "We watched all kinds of battles between the various factions across the river in Mexico. It was a strange kind of fighting. It was like a war on an eight-hour day. They would kill three or five, and at five o'clock the fighting stopped. The Yaqui Indians were the toughest. They would advance in waves. When one fell, another would take his place."

Essing, later a captain in the Army, thought that Gen. John J. Pershing was sent to the border to enhance his chances of becoming commander of the American armies. He was right. "Black Jack" Pershing would command the American Expeditionary Force during World War I.

(September 4, 1980/June 12, 1975)

Relations with the Panamanians
. . . were pretty good.

The Panama Canal Zone is a special place for Lloyd E. Brewer. It was his first home. He had never really had a home as a child.

"I was five years old when my mother died. My father put us six kids in an orphanage in Pennsylvania. I was raised by foster parents all over the country, anywhere they needed cheap labor," he said.

Then he attended the Thaddeus Stevens Trade School and learned carpentry and house design. Unfortunately, it was 1933 and there were no jobs to be had anywhere. By luck, he was accepted in the Army and assigned to the 33rd Infantry in Fort Clayton near the Miraflores Locks on the Pacific side of the canal.

"We walked our posts along the locks, and when the fleet was coming through, it was two hours on and two hours off until all the ships passed through. It would usually take two days."

The Army was on frequent maneuvers, defending itself from its own guys pretending to be the enemy, and firing blanks. However, the post became strictly spit-and-polish military during three times that President Franklin D. Roosevelt passed through the canal.

"He was the first president to go the length of the canal on a boat. I remember that at the reviews conducted for him, he was well enough to walk with assistance of a cane and the arm of a military aide."

Brewer recalls that relations with the Panamanians in those days were pretty good. They made a living off the soldiers.

"Our main problem was the civilian American population. They would have nothing to do with peacetime soldiers. They wanted to make sure they kept their daughters away from us. Once a couple invited me and a buddy to dinner. We were in civilian clothes at the time. We showed up for dinner in uniform, and they closed their blinds so the neighbors wouldn't see they had soldiers in the house."

The soldier was paid $21 a month. But he could contribute 20 cents a month to the company fund and never have to pull KP duty. The San Bias Indians did all the dirty work. The main problem was having nothing to do. Fort Clayton became known as "the suicide post" because so many soldiers took their lives.

"Our company didn't have that problem. We'd chip in and pay nine cents a gallon to fill up an old truck and go exploring. We had a lot of fun."

He recalled that an American newspaperman wrote a story about the high rate of suicide and the camp commander ordered his arrest for libel. July the Fourth Boulevard separated Balboa and Panama City. They faked an accident with a child. When the reporter crossed the street to help, he was arrested. There was a sensational trial.

"I don't remember how it came out, but things around the fort got a lot better," he said.

Brewer, who came to Corpus Christi to rebuild homes after Hurricane Celia and decided to stay, is now partially retired.

He pulled out his Army photo album. There were pictures of old ships, the locks, Roosevelt, marching troops, old biplanes, and young soldiers. It was an era when America courted the good will of Latin Americans and they responded.

So Brewer wouldn't like to see anything change.

"People today shouldn't decide something for people that far ahead of time. The canal has benefited all nations. If we let them have it back, the other nations should participate in the cost of building a bigger canal that will handle larger ships of all nations."

(September 9, 1977)

The War To End All Wars

Photo courtesy of Abe Yeager

Aerial warfare in World War I was fought by biplanes with open cockpits, like the one pictured above.

His name was P. Steele. He was an Englishman and a soldier. That's all I know about his identity. Yet I shared his thoughts and feelings about a war three quarters of a century ago.

Some time ago someone found a little address book two and a quarter by three and a half inches in some antique furniture, apparently shipped from Great Britain. Inside was an abbreviated journal covering the period 1916-1919.

At a casual glance I thought the soldier was American. But the dates are European style. Transcribing the notes, I found he was English. He was drafted at Chester, attended lineman's and signalman's schools, and in 1918 was sent to Belgium, where he found himself in the trenches around Ypres.

There is little description of actual fighting. Combat references are typically understated. In school he reported, "Zeppelin raid. Many airships. Many bombs dropped." In Belgium he mentions the almost daily air raids and "strafing" by heavy German artillery but seldom gives detail. Trench warfare was a muddy, cold, wet, nasty business. Through artillery barrages, poison gas attacks, patrol clashes, he records the type of billet that was available.

"Conditions far from ideal. Trenches full of water. No dugout," he wrote in September 1918. Then he was billeted in a hut. "Air raids every night, otherwise, 'cushy,'" he said.

In another trench there were "strafes daily and nightly by Jerry 6-inch and 9-inch and gas," but the dugout was "par bon." In relieving another unit he referred to the dugouts in the trenches as "rat holes." He carried a signal lamp into no-man's land to contact an artillery observation post "for the morrow's stunt. Tried the lamp without dimming discs, then lights WITH. Shells dropped too close to be pleasant. BDE the Signal Officer is an ass to say Jerry can't see you." He tells of a British artillery barrage that drove the Germans back and of a French cavalry charge.

He was sarcastic about the accommodations in a captured German pillbox that was "full of water and other things." They pumped and bailed to no avail. "As a result we had to wade inside and select a bedstead luxuriously appointed. Smell was high, but otherwise not too bad." He compared it to accommodations of the night before that were warm and dry. "The only drawback being the remains of several horses and cows long since deceased gassing strongly."

He was disgusted with a chore of transporting supplies through the lines. "Cheerful experience," he noted. "Pitch dark, umpteen thousand shell holes and miles of barbed wire, and also raining heavily. Nearly kicked passing through transport lines by ill-tempered mules and strafed by Jerry artillery."

Apparently the mules bothered him more than the exploding shells. Bodies and wreckage in no man's land he referred to with bitter irony as "many cheerful sights." He complimented the marksmanship of German artillery for knocking down a row of cottages near the British command post. He mentions heavy casualties from artillery and gas among both his company and civilians. A night patrol or "stunt" netted several captured Germans. He complained of having to attend signal classes when his unit pulled back for a rest. Troops removed from the lines and apparently safe were killed by exploding shells from long-range, rail-mounted naval cannon.

As a signalman, Steele received word of the Armistice. The inn was so crowded he couldn't get in. There were ceremonial parades, and when the corps commander came for a ceremonial inspection, Steele did not attend. "Too cushy on the front," he explained.

He arrived home and was back at work the next day.

I wonder what happened to P. Steele, author of that shirt pocket history of a very dirty war.

(January 15, 1988)

'I will sure be glad when they get through fighting over here...'

Just about anything can and does end up in the police stolen property section. Shelves are cluttered with merchandise police have recovered from thieves or found abandoned.

"Most of it is routine," Sgt. A. W. "Bull" Gamez said, "but we found something you might be interested in."

"We figure it was taken in a burglary in Saxet Heights. A lot of old people live there. Somebody thought there might be money in it," Sgt. Joe Farkas said. "When they found it contained only photographs and letters, they dumped it. Someone kept them all these years and probably would like to get them back."

The aluminum case had been pried open. Inside were letters and cards, all written during World War I by Pfc. Claude J. Smith to his sister, Mrs. Ed (Ella) Stanford of Sherman. There was a photograph of a young soldier and several pictures of young women. A 1963 photograph shows the man and a woman, both up in years.

The cards show pictures of scenery in France. The letters are typical of a soldier's, written with the knowledge they would be censored. His choice of subjects was limited.

"It's against the rules to tell what we are doing or where we are at," he wrote early in 1918, "but you know what I came over here for. Well, that's what I'm doing. It's quite different from the job I had at home."

Some of the envelopes are stamped, but most were sent postage-free with the writer marking "soldier's mail."

"I will sure be glad when they get through fighting over here," he wrote in the summer of 1918. "It seems that's all they know. But one thing is certain, it can't last always."

By September he had moved to a job helping run a troop train "100 miles from where the big things are happening," he wrote to ease his sister's worry about his safety. But the job was to keep him in France for nearly another year, carrying troops on their way home to seaports.

He wrote on YMCA stationery that urged soldiers to save by writing on both sides of the paper and the folks back home to save by investing in Liberty Bonds and War Savings Stamps. Twenty-five-cent U.S. Savings Stamps in a book would have been exchanged for a War Savings Certificate when it was full.

Smith never got seasick on the troopship. In the chow line he asked in a loud voice if another soldier wanted his bacon. He got all the bacon he wanted as the others suddenly decided their stomachs wouldn't take it.

He was anxious to get home, he wrote from camp in New Jersey, saying all his uniforms were wrinkled after being packed for the voyage home.

"I don't care what I look like now that I'm back. I don't intend to have them on only about five minutes after I get home. Have my blue serge suit fixed for me.

"Hey, sis, you may have to have my shoes stretched a little. I don't know if I can get them on or what. My feet has spread out like a web-footed duck. It will be a relief to have light shoes instead of hobnails."

He was on his way to Camp Pike, Arkansas, to be separated from the service. He signed the letter with X's for all the girls.

"Those letters wouldn't mean a thing to anyone else. But to some family they are a keepsake," Farkas said.

They are a little out of place in stolen property.

(February 20, 1984)

'Then they held the funeral and fired a final military salute. And the war was on again.'

The war on a section of the Western Front stopped. By mutual agreement the British and Germans quit fighting to honor a dead hero, Manfred von Richthofen.

Dr. Belo Stone, who was closing out nearly half a century as a physician in Robstown, Texas, was an Army Air Corps ground crewman attached to a British fighter squadron on that day in April 1918, seven months before the Armistice.

"The Red Baron was shot down and killed over our lines. The British conducted the funeral. Von Richthofen's entire squadron was allowed to fly over. Each plane dropped a funeral wreath over the grave. Then they held the funeral and fired a final military salute. And the war was on again," he said.

"A Canadian pilot (Capt. Roy Brown) is generally given credit for shooting the Baron down. I've never seen it written, but the Australian gunners on the ground were sure they were the ones who did it."

The Red Knight of Germany, by Floyd Gibbons, credits Brown with the kill. *The Day the Red Baron Died*, by Dale Titter, says ground gunners did it.

Stone joined the Air Corps after he graduated from Robstown High School in 1916.

"The Army didn't have many planes—maybe six or seven JN-4s. The Canadians were at war so they trained us. We went to Camp Kelly in San Antonio, then to Ontario. But it was so cold the planes couldn't fly and we were back in Texas outside Fort Worth. We nearly froze to death there. In a month we were on the front lines. We were assigned to the Royal Navy, the RAF, the Canadians, and the Australians. There were no flying fields or anything, just any field as near to the front as we could get.

"The last big push by the Germans put us into retreat. We kept moving the planes out until we were in Dunkirk. We would have been pushed into the sea except for the first American drive at Chateau Thierry. That caused the Germans to pull back, and we were saved.

"Those pilots didn't have parachutes. Observers in balloons did, and they could bail out. But when a plane caught fire, pilots just jumped out rather than burn up."

He joined an American squadron equipped with new Spads for the final two battles of the war.

After the war he attended school in France, still in the Army. He came home in August 1919, just in time to be called to duty in September when ex-soldiers were asked to volunteer their services after a major hurricane devastated much of the city of Corpus Christi.

"I got out my uniform and did police duty on North Beach for two weeks. There wasn't much left out there."

Although he fulfilled his life's ambition to be a doctor, Stone also took a fling at flying.

"I flew a lot and thought I was pretty good," he said. "Then I had a narrow escape that showed me I wasn't as good as I thought I was, so I gave it up."

(January 30, 1979)

Fortino Treviño cut hair all the way to England, then on the way to France.

Fortino Treviño, an Alice barber since 1910, used his razor and clippers to cut quite a swath through World War I. Treviño was born in New Collins, Nueces County, Texas, in 1891. The same village is now the city of Alice in Jim Wells County.

"Population was about fifteen, not counting a lot of mesquite trees," he said. The railroad passing through town was Nationales de Mexico, later to become Tex-Mex and then Texas Mexican.

There were big excursions to Corpus Christi, $1 round trip. On February 22 there were big excursions to Laredo, where dancing and partying all night marked the two border cities' international celebration of George Washington's birthday.

Treviño fought in five World War I battles. In addition to fighting, he cut hair all the way to England, then again on the way to France. A motorcycle messenger with a passenger sidecar once called for him at the front and summoned him to headquarters.

"Gen. Allen needed a haircut. I cut his hair and all of his staff's. My daddy told me to get a good French razor if I was in Paris. I asked the general if I could go to Paris. He gave me a thirty-day pass. Capt. Ream couldn't believe they would let anyone go to Paris."

The 360th Infantry went over the top at St. Mihiel in 1918. A young mail clerk was hit by machine-gun bullets, and Treviño threw him over his back and carried him to an aid station.

"I never saw him again until about fifteen or twenty years after the war," Treviño said. "I was giving a customer a shave when Scott Peters came into the shop with the president of the Frost National Bank. He picked me up and swung me around and said, 'If it hadn't been for this man, I wouldn't be alive.'

"He was a banker at Ozona and still lives there. I asked, 'What about a loan?' He said, 'You name the amount.' I said I was kidding."

He is proud of a picture preserved on a plate of himself as a soldier with a small German girl. He fed and cared for her for four months in Germany after the war until a home for her could be found.

He didn't earn many medals, but he does display an Iron Cross and combat ribbons he took from the body of a German officer. He is proud of his service and groups he helped organize. A place of honor in his shop is accorded to Alonso S. Perales, who with José Luz Saenz and José T. Canales was a prime mover in the organization of the League of United Latin American Citizens.

He noted changes in the country.

"Back in World War I we didn't feel the pride in America," he said. "They still called us Mexicans. Only about 2 percent of our people went to the war. By World War II the feelings had changed and 90 per cent of our boys served for the love of their country. All three of my sons were in the service."

(March 19, 1975)

The Big War had ended and there would never be another.

There were two separate armistices in World War II, and I remember them both. The first was V-E Day. I was three days out of San Francisco. The second was V-J Day. That was the end of the war. If Armistice Day 1918 was a bigger blast, I'm glad I wasn't there. I don't think I could have stood it.

At precisely 11 a.m. on November 11, 1918, as directed by Marshal Ferdinand Foch, guns on the Western Front fell silent, and the world exploded into the noisiest celebration in history. The Big War had ended and there would never be another. The war to end all wars was over. It was truly a time for rejoicing. There was dancing in the streets, kissing, and firing of guns and fireworks in cities all over the world. The celebration lasted for days.

President Woodrow Wilson proclaimed November 11 as Armistice Day in 1919 to remind Americans of the tragedy of war. Federal law made it a legal holiday in 1938.

In those days at 11 a.m. on November 11 in every small town across the nation, firehouse sirens sounded and factory whistles blew in the cities to remind Americans to stop and pay silent homage to the nation's war dead.

Speeches were impassioned and long—usually longer than July 4 speeches. I was young, but I couldn't help but be impressed by the speech of John Lee Smith, then a candidate for Texas lieutenant governor. He insinuated that no one could be qualified for office who had not "buried the body of a buddy in a bloody blanket."

Speeches were accompanied by parades and barbecues. Kids didn't think much about dead veterans at such events.

After World War II the civilian populations of the New England states were as happy to celebrate as the armed forces were. It was a real party.

But postwar sentiment wasn't the same as that after World War I. Nobody had the idea that the war had ended wars and the world was safe for democracy.

Nations were still facing each other over gun barrels. And somehow remembering later got confused with the abhorrence of unpopular wars. Few wanted to remember any war or the men who paid for them with their lives. [In 1954 Armistice Day was changed to Veterans Day.]

And on Veterans Day a few people will gather to hear speeches and taps by the American Legion. There will be some old veterans and maybe a few survivors who remember.

They say Veterans Day is to honor the living now. But the old veterans will still think of it as Armistice Day and turn to the west at 11 a.m. and remember.

(November 6, 1979)

Flags at City Hall
and the Courthouse
were lowered to half staff . . .

Pvt. Benjamin Birmingham received quite a homecoming on September 4, 1921. It was also his funeral. He was the first Corpus Christi soldier to die in World War I. He was killed on June 6, 1918, but was carried as missing in action for a long time.

This probably explains the oversight in that his name does not appear on the markers or the American Legion Plaque at the top of the Bluff in front of Corpus Christi Cathedral, where the other Corpus Christi men killed in the Great War are honored.

Birmingham and his brother Albert went to San Antonio and joined the Regular Army when the United States entered the war. They said they wouldn't feel like Americans if they didn't. They separated and were never to see each other again.

Benjamin made local news when his troop transport, the SS *Tuscania*, was torpedoed off the coast of Ireland early in 1918. He was one of the survivors. The next report was that he was missing in action. His mother prayed "that he had not made the supreme sacrifice but rather was a prisoner of the Germans."

Another Corpus Christian, Ernest Gragg, a member of the Navy armed guard aboard the steamship *Lochester*, went down when his ship was torpedoed. The first American Legion Post in the city, No. 81, was named for him.

Then the war was over. Cpl. Albert Birmingham wrote home. He said he had not seen nor heard from his brother "Been." He spelled phonetically, saying he had "dune sum hard fitting (fighting), and on the next drive, we throwed a big broge (barrage) on Verdun. Ours, and blew me down some. We never stop shutting at the enemy."

He said he was looking forward to dancing, asked his brother Ben not to sell his car until he could drive it, and asked about his little black horse. And, "tell my girl that I still think of her."

He lived to old age.

The flags at City Hall and the Courthouse were lowered to

half staff three years after Ben's death when his body was among the thousands the Army brought home from France.

A big crowd assembled for the funeral procession. It was led by the flag-draped casket on a caisson pulled by a Maxwell P. Dunne hearse, followed by a color guard, a Boy Scout band playing "Nearer My God to Thee," an honor escort, pallbearers, and Legionnaires in full uniform. Then came the Legion Auxiliary, the Rotary, the Kiwanis, the Elks Club, and most of the rest of the town marching in silence.

At Rose Hill Cemetery Pvt. Benjamin Birmingham, K Company, 23rd Infantry, was buried with full military honors, speeches, prayers, a 21-gun salute, "Taps," and the playing of "The Star Spangled Banner."

In the 1920s the county, the Gold Star Mothers, and the American Legion set up a memorial on the Bluff overlooking Corpus Christi Bay. There is a monument with a plaque listing all the World War I dead. There is another tower which was to have been an "eternal light." And small markers for each of the dead are spaced along the Bluff, just below the banister. Birmingham's niece, Mrs. Alfred C. Smith, is trying to rectify the error made when her uncle's name was omitted.

I've had inquiries from various veterans' groups about restoring this monument. Now that the relatives who remember those men grow fewer in number, I'd hope some of them sponsor a remodeling program to coincide with the Bluff improvement project. And while they're at it, maybe they can include the name of Pvt. Benjamin Birmingham, the first Corpus Christi soldier to die in World War I.

(July 24, 1986)

[Editor's Note: In 2001 a new memorial replaced the original version, and it includes the name of Pvt. Benjamin Birmingham.]

. . . the first military flight in the United States occurred on a nearby parade field . . .

He seemed to decide it was time to go. And in a very few days my father-in-law, Abe Yeager, was dead. Old people can do that, the doctor said. When they feel it is time to die, they die. And there's nothing to be done.

The only request he had ever made was that he be buried in the National Cemetery at San Antonio among many of his old friends with whom he had served in World War I or the Army Reserve or worked as a military reporter. That seemed appropriate enough.

Only a handful of his old friends showed up for the funeral. That would have suited him fine. He wouldn't have liked a crowd. Many friends had died or moved away since he retired twenty-five years ago. The Post Chapel was the ideal spot for the services. Flags of the states hang below the chapel dome. The walls are decorated with the regimental standards and division insignias of Army units that have served at Fort Sam Houston.

Most appropriate of all was a plaque near the entrance. It has a picture of a plane built by the Wright Brothers with the notation that the first military flight in the United States occurred on a nearby parade field, then a mesquite patch. Other officers had flown with the Wrights, but this was the first flight with an Army man at the controls.

He was Lt. Benjamin D. Foulois, flying a Wright Flyer biplane. The date was March 2, 1910. The parade field is named Gen. Arthur MacArthur Field for the father of Gen. Douglas MacArthur.

That shaky first flight at Fort Sam Houston lasted only a few minutes, but it was the beginning of the aeronautic section of the Army Signal Corps, forerunner of the Army Air Service and eventually of the United States Air Force.

Later, after reading the air corps plaque, we moved to the cemetery. It was a wet, gray day, and as the minister was concluding the brief ceremony at the graveside, there was the rumble of a military jet hammering down through the overcast. We had gone from the Wright Brothers to the jet age in a matter of minutes.

There was silence as they folded the flag and handed it to his widow. There was no bugle. It was just as well. "Taps" for Abe Yeager came from the scream of a jet engine. He wouldn't have asked for anything more.

After Yeager retired in 1955 from a long career as military writer in San Antonio, he wrote one last article, for the *Houston Chronicle*. The headline was "I Covered That Billy Mitchell Statement."

Yeager's proudest possession was an autographed picture General Mitchell gave to him in 1925. Mitchell, air commander in World War I, was the Army's ranking military aviator, but he fell from favor early in 1925 and was transferred to Fort Sam Houston as a colonel. There were no press officers or press conferences in those days. Reporters went from office to office digging out news.

"Billy Mitchell became a fertile news source on my beat and echoes of the controversy centering on him and the underlying service jealousies came to me from both ground and flying officers," Yeager wrote. "Fort Sam Houston officers informed me Mitchell's campaign for a separate air force was motivated by personal ambition so he could step up as its commander. An artillery colonel said military aviators were 'nothing but air chauffeurs who know nothing of military tactics and are incapable of command. Their chief ambition is to fly around the country and have a good time.'"

Therefore the Army would keep a tight rein on them. Airmen complained that Mitchell was the only colonel in the air service. The infantry and field artillery were top-heavy with rank that should have gone to flying officers.

Mitchell escaped injury in a crash at Dodd Field at Fort Sam Houston. The next day his book *Winged Defense* was released without War Department authorization.

"Aviators are the only persons competent to tell what is wrong and they are going to tell," Mitchell said.

After the Navy lost a flying boat and the dirigible *Shenandoah*, Miitchell blasted the lack of a governing body for the air forces. Of his career he said, "No matter what happens to any individual, the people must be roused to the dangers facing the country as the outgrowth of the bungling attitude of Army and Navy bureaucrats towards aeronautics and flyers."

Three days later he handed Yeager a copy of his sensational charges that would lead to his court-martial.

"These accidents are the direct result of the incompetency, criminal negligence and almost treasonable administration of the national defense by the Navy and War Departments," Mitchell said.

"All aviation policies are dictated by non-flying officers . . . The lives of airmen are being used merely as pawns in their hands . . ."

Airmen were sent to out-of-the way places to prevent their telling the truth.

"The bodies of my former companions in the air molder under the soil in America, Asia, Europe and Africa . . . a great many sent there by official stupidity . . ."

He told Yeager he expected to be under arrest, which "would bring the issue of national defense to a head." He dared the brass to court-martial him.

On September 19, 1925, Mitchell was relieved of duty and called to Washington as a witness before a special board on aeronautics appointed by President Calvin Coolidge. A general court-martial was convened in October. Among members of the military court was Douglas MacArthur, whom Yeager considered unfair and self-serving. Mitchell was found guilty and suspended from the service. He resigned and continued the fight as a civilian, sacrificing career for principle.

Yeager, a witness in the trial, wrote, "Methods adopted by Billy Mitchell . . . may be open to censure, but there is no longer doubt as to the accuracy of his claims."

(January 3, 1975/August 16, 1982)

Pearl Harbor

Photo courtesy of R. A. Martin
A Japanese pilot's view of Pearl Harbor's Battleship Row on December 7, 1941

"The general quarters bell was going 'Clang! Clang! Clang!' Me and another guy were waiting to go ashore. I said, 'Their drill ain't going to get me to dirty up these dress whites.' We kept waiting. The bell kept ringing. They blew a bugle and a bosun's pipe. The speaker said, 'Man your battle stations! This is no drill! This is no drill!' Something went 'Whump! Whump!' real loud.

"We stepped out on the after deck and a Japanese torpedo plane passed about thirty yards over us. He was shaking all over because he was shooting a machine gun at us. We fell back in the hatch. We went to our turret, but you don't use eight-inch guns for anti-aircraft, so we tore down the awnings we had put up for Sunday morning church services."

Albert Johnson and his shipmates on the cruiser *New Orleans* had a better view of the attack on Pearl Harbor than they wanted.

"We were across the stream from Battleship Row. The first wave was torpedo bombers. I saw the *Arizona* go. It was like the pictures of the atom bomb. It just broke in two.

"We had 1.1 millimeter cannons and machine guns. The 1.1's kept jamming. We were tied up next to the big hammerhead crane. Some Hawaiian workers were on it. They started down and bullets from the planes and from the ships were hitting all around them. They started up, then down. Some of these things seem comical now, but they weren't then. Some of our 5-inch shells may have landed in Honolulu.

"The *San Francisco* was across the dock from us, unloaded for repairs. We started passing 5-inch ammo across the dock. The guys were getting tired, and we knew the Japanese were coming back.

"I saw Chaplain Howell Forgy (Lt. j.g.) down on the dock, patting the guys on the back and talking to them. I couldn't hear. Later I learned he was yelling, 'Praise the Lord and pass the ammunition!' It wasn't long before the song 'Praise the Lord and Pass the Ammunition' came out. Later the skipper had a press conference and made Forgy answer questions so people would know who said it.

"Later, when we had thirty-six feet of our bow blown off at Guadalcanal and lost 222 men, I told the chaplain, 'looks like they got us this time.' He said, 'No, they haven't. God's on our side.' And we made it, too. The chaplain had a stroke and died in 1972.

"At Pearl Harbor the dive bombers dropped one bomb between us and a big fleet tanker loaded with aviation fuel. It had four PT Boats on its deck. If it had been hit, the whole harbor would have gone. Another bomb hit near our stern and damaged a screw. I saw the Destroyer *Shaw* go. It went in a big flash and a puff of smoke. The *Okie* just rolled over on its side.

"I was watching a launch go through the flames to pick up men from the *Oklahoma* and *Arizona*. A light cruiser was backing down and dumped them all in the water. A lot of the wounded drowned.

"Sailors who didn't know how to run launches were crashing into the liberty landing. Three days later I saw a dead Japanese pilot in the water. We tied a line around his foot, and they pulled him up at the sub base. At dark they said six Navy planes were coming in. They went overhead. Down the line a machine gun opened up. The whole harbor exploded. All six planes were shot down."

Johnson, who joined the Navy in 1940 with three friends, served fifty-six months at sea and was in thirteen engagements.

"It all happened in about two hours," he said of the Pearl Harbor attack. "Then it seemed like forever. Four years ago I went back to Pearl on the anniversary. It was the closest I've come to taking a drink since I quit twenty years ago. You don't forget."

(December 7, 1981)

They were dying without knowing that a war had started.

The attack was doubly jarring to soldiers, sailors, and Marines who had been out on the town on a Saturday night celebration. The crash of bombs and the chatter of machine guns were burned into their consciousness, and they were dying without knowing a war had started.

Over at Schofield Barracks things weren't all that hectic. Simon Gutierrez heard a lot of cussing about the Navy conducting maneuvers on a Sunday morning when everybody needed to sleep.

A plane whined down practically on the rooftop.

"What the hell, don't those guys know it's Sunday?" someone shouted.

"We heard explosions in the distance," Gutierrez said. "We saw smoke in the distance. Then Japanese planes making a run over Hickam Field turned back to make sure no planes were able to take off and get to them. That's when we saw the markings and knew they were Japanese planes.

" 'My God, they're shooting at us,' someone else yelled.

"We could see the planes exploding and burning at Hickam across the way. We couldn't see Pearl Harbor because of a hill. But we could see fire and smoke. On the second run they started strafing our barracks. I don't remember if anyone was hit or not. There wasn't much damage. But the Japanese planes were so low we could see the pilots waving goodbye to us.

"The captain came and ordered the lock broken on the supply room and guns were issued. We set up machine guns before the last attack. There was a lot of shooting, but I couldn't say any of the Japanese planes were hit.

"I joined the Army August 3, 1941, went to Fort Leonard Wood, Missouri, then arrived in Hawaii five days before the attack. We were terrified because we didn't know what to do. That night was bad, too. Everyone was scared and nervous. Every time there was a noise, everyone started shooting. Remember, there was no television then to tell us what was going on.

"If the Japanese had landed one transport of troops, they could have taken the island easily. We put dynamite on the highway in case the Japanese came ashore. We stayed there seven days. All the Japanese-Americans working in the PX or moving supplies were kicked out. We had a lot of American-Japanese soldiers with us. They were all born in the Hawaiian Islands. I had a lot of friends among them. They took that bunch and sent them to fight in Europe. They were good soldiers and lost a lot of men."

Gutierrez caught up with the war on Guadalcanal, where casualties in the outfit were heavy.

"You've heard of Condition Red?" he asked. "That was Condition Black. The Japanese put all their airplanes up and threw everything they had at us."

Later he was in the Philippine Campaign, using a bulldozer to clear supply roads through the jungle to the front lines.

"I saw things there so horrible I never talk about them," he said. "When I remember those terrible things, I can't find it in my heart to fully trust the Japanese, even today.

"I made four campaigns, was in the Army four years and four days, and never got a scratch until right before the war was over. I was supervising construction of a bridge on Luzon when a cable snapped and an I-beam fell on my toe. The rest of my outfit left when I was in the hospital. But I was sent back on a hospital ship. I had clean quarters, three squares a day, and a movie every night. I didn't get back to my home in Laredo until the war was over."

But the biggest surprise of all was still when a nineteen-year-old kid woke up that Sunday morning at Schofield Barracks to find bullets flying toward him from an enemy he didn't know he had.

(December 7, 1982)

'The first wave hit us and was on its way to Pearl in a matter of minutes.'

The guys in C. W. Mallard's outfit were the first to know that the Japanese were attacking Pearl Harbor this day in 1941. Mallard, naturally called "Duck" by his friends, was attached to a patrol squadron of PBYs, the lumbering seaplanes that were the Navy's eyes early in the war. The base was at Kaneohe, on the windward side of the Hawaiian island of Oahu, over the mountains to the west of Honolulu and Pearl Harbor.

"We were up early that Sunday morning playing a game of football," he said. "I was resting in my sack in the barracks when it hit. We couldn't figure out what was making all that noise. I looked out and saw planes. My first thought was 'Air Corps, on a practice run. Crazy sonuvaguns. They're messing around with live ammo in the bay where our planes are tied up. Someone ought to tell them.'

"Then a plane banked around the barracks, and I saw those big red balls on the wings. It took a second for the shock to hit me. Japan! War! I took off running for the hangar.

"Old John, our ordnance chief, was handing out 50-caliber machine guns. We grabbed ammunition from the middle of the hangar, and we were firing in a matter of a very few minutes. First guns in operation were aboard the planes, but we had to move from there after the planes were set on fire.

"Japanese planes came in waves. First were the Zeros, then bombers, then fighters and another wave of bombers. The first wave hit us and was on its way to Pearl in a matter of minutes. They were hit before any warning could be sounded.

"We weren't able to get any planes in the air. We had about thirty-six planes in three squadrons. Some were in the water. The rest were on the ramps. We were only able to salvage one of those and that took two months. That's how torn up they were.

"We had one patrol plane out. It was two and a half hours out when the attack came. Their course hadn't brought them in contact with the Japanese or there might have been some warning.

"It seemed like the attacks lasted all day, but they couldn't have been more than an hour. Luckily, they concentrated on the new hangar. It was still under construction and didn't have much in it. Our ammunition was in the old hangar.

"One of our guys was killed and some others were hit. One kid was blown into a building and hurt real bad. I don't know if he lived or not. We kept shooting. I don't know how many hits we made. We shot down one Zero. It crashed in a place where it wouldn't hurt anybody—the officers' barracks—only kidding."

Duck was on Midway Island during the battle there. The PBYs fared better that time. One spotted the Japanese fleet far out to sea, but the base buildings and fuel tank were destroyed by Japanese bombers.

His squadron was in every campaign through the Battle of the Philippines. He retired from the Navy after twenty years. During our telephone conversation I asked him how to spell "Kaneohe."

"Gollee, man," he answered. "That was thirty-eight years ago."

(December 7, 1979)

The *Jarvis* seemed to have a charmed life . . .

Charles Ramsey is a lucky fellow. All of his shipmates aboard the destroyer *Jarvis* perished in the battle of Guadalcanal. He survived. But when Pearl Harbor was attacked that fateful Sunday morning forty-five years ago, the *Jarvis* seemed to have a charmed life in the middle of the holocaust caused by Japanese bombers and torpedo planes.

"One feller got hit in the leg by a .25-caliber bullet, but the doctor pulled it out with a pair of tweezers," Ramsey recalled. "I was topside when the attack started. A chief boatswain yelled that we were being attacked by the Japanese. About then a plane flew by and we saw the big red balls on the wings, and we saw smoke and heard explosions on Battleship Row.

"I went back and helped man a 5-inch gun until the regular crew got there. Then I grabbed up a Browning automatic rifle and started shooting at the planes when they came over. I could see where my shots were going because every fifth bullet was a tracer, but I don't think I hit anything.

"There was this big, tall crane at the end of the dock. That kept the dive bombers from coming at us. But when they had made their runs on the battleships, they sort of stalled and we got some good shots at them. It was strange. When one of them was hit, a sort of yellowish, black smoke came out of them before they crashed in the harbor.

"I had a ringside seat at the battle. We were waiting to go into dry dock where the *Pennsylvania* and the destroyer *Shaw* were. The *Shaw* was the one which exploded within a big ball of fire that shows up in the pictures of Pearl Harbor. Then the high-level bombers came over. They were two-engine planes. The bombs were actually 16-inch armor-piercing shells with fins welded on the back to keep them from tumbling. This is what hit the *Arizona* and the *Oklahoma*. One went down the stack of the *Arizona* and blew it up. One went through the 12-inch steel deck of the *Oklahoma* and sank it.

"I saw the *Arizona* blow up and I saw the *Oklahoma* roll over.

The cruiser *Helena* was docked behind us. The mine layer *Oglala* was tied up alongside it. A torpedo bomber hit the *Oglala*. They cast it loose, and it drifted alongside us and sank. A bomb blew off the fantail of the *Helena*. All this time Jap planes were coming down the alley to reach the battleships. They flew right past us, and we had a lot of shots at them.

"It took us an hour and a half to get up steam. We went to sea right away, but the battle was pretty well over then. We had returned from taking supplies to Wake, Johnson, and Midway islands and had not refueled, since we were going in dry dock.

"About twenty-five miles from Pearl Harbor we met the aircraft carrier *Enterprise*. How the Japs failed to find her, I don't understand. With her were the heavy cruisers *Astoria*, *Quincy*, and *Vincennes*. That's all the fleet we had left, and they weren't ready to fight at that time.

"We looked for the Japanese fleet for three days. By then we were riding three feet above our waterline. We were on empty when we got back to Pearl. We came back to the West Coast for refitting. I was reassigned to the USS *Taylor*. The *Jarvis* had its bow blown off in the Guadalcanal invasion.

"As it was being towed at sea, two Japanese cruisers found her and sank her with all hands. I knew nearly everyone aboard her by their first names. It hurt."

The *Taylor* went through most of the Pacific war battles unscathed. Ramsey had joined the Navy in 1940.

"After Pearl Harbor we figured we on the *Jarvis* were lucky," he said. "I guess I was the only real lucky one. It still hurts."

(December 5, 1986)

'It couldn't have lasted too long, but it seemed forever.'

He had another name, but even some of his friends thought it was Chief. He was just "Chief." Much of his life was spent in the Navy, a lot of it as a chief petty officer. When he started his own business, it was called Chief's Moving and Storage. And a good part of his business came from Navy men on the move.

Thomas Lee McDonel died the other day. That was the name he concealed so well. His was a quick smile, and his generous nature was such that people often took advantage of him. When they did, he never got angry. He met it with a shrug and a grin.

I don't know how many times I listened to his sea stories, but I never tired of them, for he was always the anti-hero. And some of his stories were humorous.

He was at Pearl Harbor that fateful December 7.

"Four of us had been to a football game Saturday afternoon between the University of Hawaii and an Oregon college. That night we went to a geisha house up the Pearl River. That wasn't a bawdy house, but we thought it was before we went up there.

"It was midnight when we left, and no taxis were running. It was 5 in the morning when we got to Mary's Landing. We caught the supply boat back to the ship [the battleship *Tennessee*]. We took off our neckerchiefs and unloaded supplies like we were in a work party. It worked. We didn't get caught coming aboard late.

"I went to my storeroom (He was a storekeeper first class at the time.) and went to sleep on a sack of beans. Some guy came in and yelled we were being bombed. Guys were always pulling something when you got back from liberty. I got up. Nobody was down there. The hatches were all battened. I decided I had better get topside. I stepped out. The air was full of smoke. Shrapnel was falling all over the decks. Men were running everywhere. Nothing but confusion.

"The smoke was from the *Arizona*. She was tied up in front of us. I couldn't get to my battle station, so I started helping with a 5-inch gun. We were firing straight up in the air, hoping we'd hit something. We couldn't see for the smoke. The range setter set some of the shells too short, and they exploded almost as soon as they left the barrel.

"We kept firing and the gun got hot. I didn't know until later that my feet were burned. I was just wearing socks."

Operating a weapon without shoes is not a good idea. Hot cartridges can raise blisters on your feet. The gun had been heavily coated with grease, since it was seldom used in peacetime, even in practice. Hot grease ran from the gun and burned his feet. That is how he got his Purple Heart, as he laughingly told the story.

"It couldn't have lasted too long," he said of the attack, "but it seemed forever. I looked back and saw the *Oklahoma* roll over. I couldn't believe it. It wasn't thirty minutes before welders were on the hull cutting holes.

"We were inboard from the *West Virginia*. She took hits from torpedo planes and went down. The crew abandoned ship and came aboard the *Tennessee* like a swarm of rats. The *Nevada* was under way. The smoke cleared and we saw a torpedo hit her and we saw her run aground.

"A plane crashed 100 yards out. That was the only plane I saw. Then it was over. I went down to sick bay with my feet, but there were so many guys in worse shape, I got some petroleum jelly and doctored myself. We only lost two men. One of them was scared to death.

"That night was crazy. They issued rifles. Someone on the island could fire a shot and everyone would start shooting. There was word that Japanese transports had landed.

"The next day we launched boats and started pulling in bodies. We would tow them to shore, and the corpsmen would pull them in and take them to the athletic field for identification. We were bringing in six to ten bodies at a time. We got a lot of bodies off the *West Virginia*."

He was still helping with the cleanup on December 18 when his six-year enlistment was up. He re-upped immediately.

"They towed the *Maryland* out of the way and we could get out. We headed for Bremerton, Washington, to be re-outfitted. I decided that battleships weren't a very good thing to be on."

Many of his stories were about how he missed out on things.

He requested duty on a ship he was told the keel was being laid for and that there would be a wait while it was built. Instead he was sent to a ship that was sailing immediately for the South Pacific. He was at the Guadalcanal-Tulagi landings in August 1942, in the Solomons, at Rendova, the Battle of Bougainville, the landing at Guam, and practically every major Pacific engagement.

All this I learned from papers he never showed anyone. Instead I heard stories about how Harold Stassen, later a presidential contender, got him stationed ashore to play on an island baseball team. His stories could have been right out of *Tales of the South Pacific*.

One of his friends, a regular Luther Billis-type of promoter, figured out a way to get real whiskey with the help of air crewmen landing on the island.

No sales were made and no whiskey drunk before the scheme was uncovered, and all the cache of booze was confiscated. He had offered to buy some of the supply and was therefore implicated though not fully guilty. It was enough to get him moved on to Australia, where he collected humorous adventures by the score.

Chief was one of those guys things naturally happened to, particularly if he had a few drinks. Therefore I have no reason to discount any of them.

But I doubt all his foul-ups. His record indicates he was 4.0 (Navy perfect) in everything he did.

One of his commanding officers wrote on his efficiency report, "He is ever looking for opportunities to better himself as is evidenced by taking his commanding officer duck hunting. It is felt that McDonel could advance more rapidly and attain better marks if he ever shoots a deer and distributes the meat to the right persons. McDonel is highly recommended as a duck hunter, but can stand improvement with regards to deer and bowling."

Even his commanding officer couldn't take Chief seriously.

Even though his papers show a grim side of the war, it is his smile a lot of us will remember—and stories like the admiral's wife's toilet seat and why an ensign scrubbed the admiral's ass, which was actually a donkey. But I couldn't very well tell that here.

(December 7, 1977/October 26, 1987)

'I said, "That's too real for a drill."'

Russell Beardsley blames the U.S. government for the sinking of the Argentine cruiser *General Belgrano* by the British. He served aboard the ship three years during World War II. It was the USS *Phoenix* before it was sold to Argentina in 1951.

"Our government didn't have any business selling our ships to little countries. You never know when one of them will be shooting back at us with our own ships," he said.

Beardsley boarded the *Phoenix* in January 1941. He was aboard her during the Japanese attack on Pearl Harbor.

"There had been a lot of drills, and when a plane came in low and dropped a bomb and a big ball of fire came up, I said, 'That's too real for a drill.' About then they sounded general quarters. The guy who had the key to the ammunition lockers was ashore on liberty. They had to break the locks off with sledgehammers before we could fire a shot. As far as I remember, we had never practiced shooting at air targets."

He had a ringside view of the attack from his battle station in the fire control tower high above the ship anchored out in the harbor. He was a range finder for the large guns, which couldn't be used against aircraft.

"I saw a plane above the *Arizona*. It looked like it was six feet above the stack when it released its bomb. I think the bomb went down the stack. That's when the ship went up. I saw the *Oklahoma* roll over and the *Shaw* explode. A torpedo plane was coming right at us. Just before it released its torpedo, it was shot down by a destroyer (the *Blue*) and crashed before it could reach us. I saw planes on the mainland crash as they tried to take off. I heard they had been sabotaged.

"I went below and saw a 3-inch gun glowing red hot. I ran to tell them it was about to blow up when the barrel wilted like spaghetti. The *Phoenix* was never hit, but I'm sure some of the shells we fired landed in town. I think we shot down some of our own planes in the panic.

"We got out of Pearl Harbor faster than any ship ever has. They said we didn't even take time to pull up the anchor. They just let the chain go and we were moving. We went to San Francisco and were fueled and fully supplied and back at sea in two days. The *Phoenix* was practically the entire Pacific Fleet at that time. We headed for Australia, where attack was expected at any time. We saw two ships on the horizon and thought it was the end. They were about the only two ships left in the Australian Navy.

"We were in the Indian Ocean when one of our scout planes landed. They hurried over and jerked it out of the water and we took off. We had almost sailed between two columns of ships into the heart of the whole Japanese fleet."

Soon the *Phoenix* joined other ships in a task force and was in a number of engagements.

"When I left it, a yeoman pulled the record. It showed forty-two torpedoes had been fired at it. None of them hit. The *Phoenix* was a good ship. You get a feeling for a ship almost like the feeling for a person.

"To know she's lying at the bottom of the sea down there makes me sick. After all those battles, they sell her to a country like Argentina. It isn't right. You'll hear a lot more complaints when the guys who served on the *Phoenix* hold a reunion this fall in San Antonio. I'll bet all the other guys feel like I do. They ought to put a ship out to pasture like they do horses who have good records.

"One thing, they named an atomic submarine *Phoenix*. The *Phoenix* still lives, even if it isn't the same ship we remember."

(May 14, 1982)

'It was an end and a start, and we were there.'

I sat down the other day with a group of men who belong to a very exclusive organization. No others may qualify for membership. They are some of the local Pearl Harbor Survivors Association, one of the few active veterans groups spawned by World War II.

"We all participated in many other battles, but Pearl Harbor was a turning point in history. It changed the lives of Americans and the world. It was an end and a start, and we were there," said Jack Connolly.

The 120,000 men at Pearl Harbor thirty-three years ago now number about 8,000, and the dinner conversation touched on heart attacks, operations, illnesses of some members. I thought of the old Civil War vets as the field began to narrow in their longevity race.

"Pearl survivors used to come through the base, but it's been too long now. They've all retired," said Jack Parsons.

There are some seventy Pearl Harbor survivors in this area, and twenty-seven belong to the association. Connolly, Parsons, Carl Hatcher, and Jesse Smith all concede they didn't do much fighting that lazy Sunday morning in 1941, for there was nothing to fight with. But they had a ringside seat at one of the most spectacular battles in history.

The guns were moved from Parsons' sea-going tug before the battle. Hatcher was in the shower on Ford Island when a 500-pound bomb hit the barracks. It didn't explode. Neither did a dud that hit a turret on the USS *Tennessee*, killing sixteen men, Smith, a Marine on the ship, said.

The *West Virginia*, moored alongside, took two torpedoes intended for the *Tennessee* and sank. The *Arizona* sank behind her and the *Oklahoma* in front of her.

Connolly was across the way on the destroyer *Thornton*, and Japanese planes nearly scraped her deck releasing torpedoes at Battleship Row. The *Thornton* was damaged by gunfire from her sister ship, which tried to train its 6-inch surface guns on the low-flying aircraft.

Shortly before the attack Parsons' brother had come aboard his ship for a visit. As they looked for guns, he noticed his brother's shoe was full of blood. He hadn't felt the shrapnel wound.

All recall pulling bodies and injured men from the water. Some were so badly burned their flesh pulled from their bones.

The suddenness and incredibility of the attack caused chaos, anger, confusion, and jitters. Several two-man Japanese submarines were sunk. The USS *Litchfield* had another sub pinned to the bottom and withdrew reluctantly when orders explained the sub was one of ours.

Several U.S. planes returning to the island were shot down by nervous gunners who were managing to get more weapons firing. And in Honolulu residents marveled at the damage they assumed was caused by hostile gunfire. It was actually misdirected gunfire as naval guns attempted to fire at the angry-gnat-like attackers.

Water was drawn from swimming pools and boiled, "and it was chicken every day for a week." Barracks became hospitals, and it was General Quarters for forty-eight hours as the battered naval base awaited the knockout punch that was never to come.

Smith had arrived at Pearl directly from sea school and boot camp. Connolly had joined the Navy in July 1941. Parsons, an old salt, had sailed the South Seas since 1936. Hatcher was a Merchant Mariner for two years before enlisting in the Navy in 1939. He arrived in Pearl Harbor the month before the attack.

All were kicked from a peaceful sleep onto a bloody deck, and the fact they survived has given them a common bond. They do not intend to let the world forget.

(December 5, 1974)

Dark Days

Photo courtesy of R. A. Martin

During a raid by Japanese bombers, smoke rising from the ruins of the targeted base illustrates the dire situation the United States and its allies faced in the early days of the Pacific war.

April 9, 1942, was the start of a horrible nightmare for Virgil Catchings. That was the day Americans in the Philippines surrendered.

Catchings, who lives near Seguin, Texas, said, "I landed at Nichols Field sixteen days before Pearl Harbor. I was crew chief for a P-40 (fighter plane). We knew something was up and worked night and day, installing new 50-caliber machine guns and getting the planes in top shape. Then came Pearl Harbor. We knew we were next. Our pilots were ready to take off when the order came from General MacArthur: 'All planes are grounded until further notice!' He said we could do nothing until war was declared.

"The bombs fell and our planes were blown up, sitting there waiting to go. Three-fourths of our planes were wiped out. Fighters strafed us and killed a lot of people and wiped out the rest of the aircraft. They handed us rifles and we became infantrymen."

They fought until they ran out of food and ammunition. The army surrendered April 9. A month earlier Catchings had been hit in the back by bomb shrapnel, and he wasn't at full strength for the ordeal that followed. It was the Bataan Death March. Those who stopped to drink muddy water or lagged behind were shot or bayoneted. Survivors staggered on as guards were relieved every few hours.

"The bodies were pushed off the side of the road. Months later we came down the road on trucks on a prison work detail. Animals had dug up the remains, and the side of the road was white with human bones," he said.

Prison life was cruel, as men were forced to run a gauntlet of guards swinging baseball bats. If anyone attempted to escape, ten others in his unit were shot. Thousands died of disease or beatings. At another camp the guards were not so cruel. They were as hungry as the prisoners.

"We were working on a landing strip, and the Japanese major's big fat dog followed us. The sergeant suggested we kill the dog. The guards supplied the extra rice, and we cooked up a real feast. That dog was delicious. The major kept whistling for his dog, and we and the guards helped him look for it," Catchings laughed.

There was no laughter on the trip to Japan. Men were packed standing up in the teeming hold of the ship. There was no room to sit or lie down. The stench was awful.

"Sewage was lifted to cans that spilled over the men below. Men became animals. Some killed their mates just for a place to lie down. About one-third died before we reached Hong Kong."

He contrived a hammock from a blanket and made his own sleeping area. Another ship was sunk by American submarines. Exploding depth charges clanged the ship's hull. Some guys traded rice for cigarettes.

"Those who smoked didn't eat and soon died," he said.

In Northern Japan his lot improved some. There was little food, but he was put to work for a kindly old blacksmith who had once lived in America. He kept Catchings posted on the progress of the war.

"He said soon I could get rid of my dirty clothes, get clothes with creases, and walk down the main street in San Francisco and order meat and potatoes."

He weighed ninety pounds when surrender came. The prisoners couldn't digest rich food. Catchings was hospitalized for a year before he returned to active duty. He served twenty-one years in the Air Force, then worked three years at a civilian job until bad health forced his retirement. His wife still awakens him when he flails and screams in his sleep. Bad dreams still come back, even after thirty-six years.

(April 9, 1980)

He earned four Silver Stars
in less than a month . . .

When bad weather is coming, Willie MacCormack doesn't have to listen to a weathercast. His body sounds the alarm. Well it should, for MacCormack, one of the most decorated living American servicemen, received several Purple Hearts as a Marine sergeant in World War II. A bayonet wound in the chest pains him most. His was the last resistance to the Japanese on Corregidor Island.

"In war movies they shoot and shoot. We had enough bullets for seven minutes, then went to the knife. I was trying to get my bayonet out of a Japanese soldier's head when the other one hit me. I got him with my knife, but he messed up my ribs."

His hip also bothers him. His pelvis was crushed by an ore truck in a Japanese slave labor camp. On Bataan a bullet went through his helmet and nearly scalped him. In his first air raid a bomb burst near him. He told his captain he needed a medic.

"Roll out from under that hot metal, and it'll quit burning you," the captain advised.

And he has other scars from a busy time when he earned four Silver Stars in less than a month in April 1942, an unequaled feat. He has about forty-eight medals and ribbons, including Bronze Stars, Letters of Commendation, China and Philippine medals, and others. He was awarded a medal last May from the Republic of China for his service there prior to World War II. He won Silver Stars, the nation's third highest medal, by:

Rescuing 123 men from a tunnel that was caving in from the explosions in an air raid;

Drawing fire of Japanese fighter planes in an open rice paddy. As a decoy he was responsible for fourteen planes being shot down;

Rescuing the crew of an artillery battery, replacing the breach in a damaged cannon, and inflicting heavy damage on a surprised Japanese division across the bay;

Saving the lives of eighty-three men trapped in a blazing powder magazine. He pried open a sealed door, wrapped himself in wet sacks, and extinguished fires, preventing the magazine from exploding.

In other action he dove into eighteen feet of water under constant enemy fire to retrieve a cargo of .50-caliber machine-gun bullets from two sunken American seaplanes to replenish Corregidor's supply of ammunition.

He led a platoon that repulsed an initial Japanese landing attempt, with heavy losses to the invaders. Troops from a fleet of landing barges were wiped out. A scar covers his left arm where he was burned when he fired a water-cooled machine gun, aiming it by resting the hot barrel on his arm as he ran towards the startled invaders, a model for later movie heroics. As Bataan was surrendering, he slipped through enemy lines and blew up the American ammunition dump.

"I used hand grenades and some dynamite to set up a chain reaction. I set it off with my rifle from 250 yards. The Japanese were really mad about that. It blew up almost a whole division."

He escaped, firing from the hip with an automatic rifle as enemy troops chased him. His captain wrote a story about that scene, and an artist illustrated the story with a picture.

"We just did what we had to do. Besides, we had our butts backed up to the water, and there was no place to swim," he said. "We didn't have anything to lose."

But he and his comrades had a lot to lose, they learned after they surrendered to the Japanese.

McCormack has told his war stories so many times at the Ingleside VFW, he has them down pretty pat. But television set him off on a new tack.

"Did you see that television show about Douglas MacArthur?" he snorted. "They had him riding to the PT Boat in a Jeep. Why, we'd never seen a Jeep. We were lined up four deep on each side and he walked down the tunnel and got on the boat. That was all there was to it."

I asked if the general awarded him his Silver Stars.

"No. He just made the announcements, put them on the bulletin board, and we went back on duty."

And tough duty it was. He and eight other Marines were among the last fighting on Corregidor when "Gen. Jonathan Wainwright walked out with a Japanese general and said, 'Stop fighting, boys. We have surrendered.'

"The Japanese combat troops were decent. They even made us tea. We hadn't had much to eat in twenty-nine days. The occupation troops were the bad ones. I was hung up by my thumbs, beaten, burned with cigarettes, and starved."

He survived the 360-kilometer death march and carried a colonel much of the way to keep him from being executed. He chopped wood, gathered soybeans, and was working in a mine when the ore cart fell on him, crushing his pelvis and hips.

"I lay there with sandbags on me for four months. The lice were eating me up. I started crawling around until I could move. I started out at 217 pounds, and after that I weighed 102 pounds."

The Marines felt he was dead. The papers for a gold leaf cluster for his fourth Silver Star were stamped "Posthumous." It was later scratched out. Near the end of the war, his message home was broadcast by Tokyo Rose, and a ham radio operator passed the message on to his parents.

"I was a prisoner 1,212 days. After we were liberated, they put me in the hospital and flew me back to Pearl Harbor, and the plane ran out of gas and had to land on the beach."

He re-enlisted and ended up in Korea.

"One day I was serving in the honor guard. When Gen. MacArthur walked by, he stopped and looked at me. He said, 'What is this man doing here? He was on Corregidor. Send him home.'"

That ended Willie's military career.

But he is ever the Marine. He keeps a clean dress blue uniform handy. He will dress up in it any time a charity wants to raise money. He wears most of his decorations, "just wear the medals someone pinned on me," he said.

He was out Saturday helping celebrate "our" (the Marine Corps') birthday and again Sunday for Veterans Day. He flies the American flag every day in front of his house. He's not able to pull in shrimp nets any more. His old wounds pain him too much.

He learned shrimping early around Aransas Pass and Ingleside, where he went to school through the sixth grade.

"The seventh grade was at Taft, and we didn't have any way to get there."

At fourteen he shipped out on a merchant ship. He joined the Marines in 1939.

"My father was a Texas Ranger. He never gave up hope I was alive. Once he played 'There's a Star-Spangled Banner Waving Somewhere' five times on a pool-hall nickelodeon. One guy told him he was tired of that song and to quit playing it. My father knocked him out cold and said, 'That song's for my boy.'

"That's the song I want them to play over my grave when I die," he said.

That's not too much for Willie McCormack to ask.

(November 12/November 13, 1979)

'It was never blown up on the ground. It was bombed by our bombers.'

The Bridge on the River Kwai, the story of how a group of British soldiers, under the leadership of their commander (Alec Guinness), built the strategic railroad only to have it destroyed by a group of British commandos, was acclaimed as an outstanding motion picture. But you'd never convince Harvey Boatman of that because he helped build that bridge—several times.

"Pure fiction," he says of the movie. "It was never blown up on the ground. It was bombed by our bombers. Once three bombs hit it and leveled it clear to the ground."

And the workers were not all British. They were Dutch, Malaysians, Americans, Australians, British, Burmese, and others.

"The British and French had attempted to build that railroad for years through the jungle and over the mountains. But they couldn't do it. The Japanese did it, though. It was an expensive railroad. They say it cost one life for every railroad tie laid down," he said.

The workers were starved, worked from sunup to sundown, and frequently beaten by their Japanese or Korean guards. Only 38 percent of the men of his battalion and survivors of the cruiser USS *Houston* lived to see the end of the war.

His was the Lost Battalion of Java. Nobody knew what happened to them until they were liberated. Also it was assumed all hands on the *Houston* had been lost. More than 500 officers and men survived.

Harvey joined the National Guard in Wichita Falls in 1940 "to beat the draft." He was assigned to the 22nd Battalion, 131st Field Artillery. It earned a reputation as a crack outfit.

"We were told we were going to the Philippines, where life was easy. We should take our tennis racquets, golf clubs, and baseball bats because garrison duty would be a breeze. We were between Pearl Harbor and the Philippines on December 7 when the Japanese attacked," he said.

Instead of heading for the Philippines, the ship turned south and landed them in Java.

"We wondered why we were landed there. After the war I kept asking why. Finally I was told we were sent on a suicide mission. The word was leaked that 80,000 Americans had landed in Java when actually there were only 500 of us. The Japanese diverted their main force from Australia to attack Java. We saved Australia and didn't even know it."

They fought with their 75-millimeter howitzers and rifles. Before the island was surrendered, Harvey was shot through the leg. "I felt a stinging and my shoe filled with blood. A .25-caliber bullet passed through my leg without hitting anything. A sergeant grabbed a machine gun and cut the tops from some palm trees. The sniper fell out and hung by the rope tying him to the tree."

After the surrender the Japanese guards and the Koreans who relieved them were brutal. The prisoners were beaten with rifle butts, prodded with bayonets, and whipped with bamboo poles. They were taken by ship to Singapore. Some ships were sunk carrying prisoners.

"A sub pulled alongside us and could hear Americans were aboard. It waited until the ship unloaded and sank it as it left the port."

The prisoners were taken to work on the railroad. In lifting heavy logs the guards figured "one elephant or ten Americans."

Disease and starvation began to take a toll. Dozens were buried daily. Some were killed by Americans bombing the railroad, which never moved much material because of the damages that the prisoners were forced to repair time and time again. Malnutrition made the men susceptible to beriberi, pelegra, malaria, dengue fever, and leprosy. Ulcers formed after a guard beat his legs, and Harvey developed gangrene and pneumonia. His companions helped him beat hopeless odds. He lived to undergo almost unspeakable hardships.

"You may think you have known hunger," he said, "but if you get hungry enough long enough, you can feel food going down your stomach. You can actually feel the energy it creates flowing into your body. You tingle all over. People say, 'I wouldn't eat that.' They don't understand that when you get hungry enough, you'll eat anything. We ate anything that moved—rats, snakes, snails."

They were fed one small bowl of wormy rice a day and whatever they could catch. Once it was a 24-foot python pulled from a thatched roof.

"We sliced it up into steaks, roasted it, made stew, and ate real good for two or three days," he said.

It was food wangled by his friends that saved his life.

Those with as many as three maladies were given up for dead. He had amoebic dysentery and pneumonia, and gangrene had set up in his leg. A Dutch doctor wanted to cut it off.

"I had seen several men who lost legs or arms. They all died within a day or two. I said I would die with my leg on."

Several others held him down while the doctor scraped away rotten flesh. There were no anesthetics. He poured hot water over his infected leg. He could see bone and tendons through the wound.

"I'd pass out, wake up and pour more water over it and squeeze it and rub and press down. One day it popped out near my ankle and all the infection ran out. After that I started to recover."

Friends slipped out of camp and brought him bananas and sugar. Then they brought him soup that gave him strength. He asked where they got the meat.

"Remember Rover?" they asked. That was a big dog that had wandered into camp. The food saved his life. He was able to return to the slave labor in the jungle.

Leeches, ticks, fleas, lice, and dozens of other pests drained the prisoners' strength. Men were beaten to death for no good reason. There was no escape, for there was no place to go and natives outside the camp would have turned them in for rewards. Bombings became more frequent. The war was winding down.

Then Harvey was stricken with appendicitis. The Dutch doctor, Han Hekking, operated on him, using a spinal injection he had concocted from jungle herbs. The operation was painless. Two days later fierce looking troops appeared. They were American paratroopers. The war was over.

The guards had fled. One particularly vicious character was "taken care of" by the prisoners. Harvey got up from his sick bed, went to the camp headquarters, and demanded red, white, and blue cloth. The guards said there was no cloth. He threatened them and they returned with cloth. Red and white were available from Japanese flags.

"I don't know where they got the blue," he said.

He cut the stars, sewed the stripes, and flew his flag over the camp along with British and Dutch flags. An officer told him if he left it flying, he would mail it to Harvey. He never did.

Two years ago as he visited the Lost Battalion Museum at Wichita Falls, he saw a crudely made little American flag. It was the one he had fashioned. Nobody could explain where it had been or how it got to the museum. Harvey is happy it is back.

Back in the States he and other survivors volunteered to do duty in Japan.

"It was our intention to reduce the population by about 20 percent," he said. "The general laughed and said there was no way we would be sent to Japan."

He says he harbors no hate for the Japanese. "I hated them for years. Then I found out hate does you no good. You can dislike, but that gets you in trouble, mentally and physically. You can push things from your mind. I could speak fluent Japanese but not now.

"It's like a bad dream that never happened. But it did something to us all. We feel things inside, but we can't express feelings."

And there were dreams. He had to get separate beds so he would not hit his wife in his sleep. He tore up pillows in the night. And the old prisoners are having health problems. Harvey has had quadruple bypass surgery. His lungs give him trouble and his leg aches constantly.

"But I still have it, so I have no complaints," he said. A little sheepishly he admits he drives a Japanese-built truck. "Can't wear one of the things out," he said.

The horrible nightmare that began forty-five years ago grows a little dimmer. And if you think the *Bridge on the River Kwai* was entertaining, don't talk to Harvey about it.

(August 10, 1987)

'There are some things I never tell. They are so bad I won't think of them.'

Joe Loya recalls the Bataan Death March and life in a Japanese prison like it was yesterday. Thirty-eight years later he still wakes up screaming, dreaming Japanese guards are chasing him. He emotionally recalled the end of the war.

"Japanese officers drove into camp, hooked up a radio, and stood at attention. There was some talk (over the radio) in Japanese. Then it said, 'This is the voice of freedom coming to you from the Battleship *Missouri* in Tokyo Bay. Here is General Douglas MacArthur. He said: 'There are no prisoners of war in the Pacific.'"

Loya's eyes flooded with tears at the recollection. "A wonderful, wonderful moment."

An American officer cautioned them to act like men who believed in democracy. He asked them not to seek revenge. But he brought out the guards so the prisoners could curse them and vent their frustration.

"There was this one guard. He beat me because I reached for a piece of radish on the ground. I was still mad at him. I'm afraid I broke the rules. I broke my crutch over his head," Loya said meekly.

The men had been beaten, starved, and humbled for more than three years. More than half their number captured on Bataan Peninsula April 9, 1942, were dead.

He was in a Civilian Conservation Corps camp when he was drafted in 1940. He was at Clark Field in Manila on December 8, 1941, (December 7 in Hawaii) when bombs rained from the sky.

"They told us not to fire. War hadn't been declared. Our planes were destroyed on the ground. We didn't think the Japanese would be there so quick and we didn't have radar. We thought their planes were ours coming to help us."

This was the beginning of his nightmare.

"We put up a good fight for three months. But we knew the Japanese were coming down the island—thousands of them. We were out of quinine and there was a lot of fever. There were no supplies and we ate horses, dogs, monkeys, and even python snakes. On March 8 General King surrendered. He said we could surrender, head for the hills, swim for Corregidor, or fight. About 600 of us dug a trench and prepared to fight. Early in the morning we heard tanks in the jungle. We didn't have anything but rifles, so we held them up and surrendered.

"Japanese soldiers searched us, looking for diamond rings and watches. They didn't want my crucifix. A Japanese officer stood on a tank and told us the Philippines had been conquered by the Imperial Army and we would pay for our crimes. He said for every bullet found on us we would be slapped one time. I had more than a hundred bullets.

"After I was hit about eight times I couldn't feel anything. Our noses and mouths were bleeding and our ears were numb and ringing. The officer said we were to be marched to San Fernando, where we would be fed and cared for. He was lying. We marched and marched. They didn't want to waste ammunition. So anytime a guy couldn't keep up, they stuck a bayonet in him. They left some sick guys in the road so trucks would squash them. Finally they told us we could stop for a drink in a creek. The water was filled with rotten bodies. They said, 'Go ahead and drink. You are thirsty.' They laughed." Loya paused. "I shouldn't do it, but I get mad all over again."

He fell silent. We were sitting on a bench in Sherill Park. The American flag popped in the wind above us. He stared across the bright bay to rest his mind from the horror. I waited for him to continue.

"I've told this story before," he said, "but there are some things I never tell. They are so bad I won't think of them."

The infamous march of death began thirty-seven years ago yesterday. I didn't press him for his personal horrors. The ones he would relate were bad enough.

"I stumbled and my helmet fell off. I reached for it and a Japanese ran at me with his bayonet. I backed off and said I didn't want the helmet. We got so tired we didn't dare sit down. If we did, we couldn't get up and they'd kill us on the spot.

"We were crazy with thirst. Then they brought through rice and water and gave us a handful of each. I never thought that raw, uncooked rice could taste so good, but it did. They told us we could rest the night, but after two hours they started us walking again. A lot of people were killed. They came by with water again. A guard got busy, and the can was at my feet. I drank and drank. It was dirty water, but I didn't care.

"They fed us sweet potato soup and gave us all the water we wanted. We all got sick. They planned that. Dysentery would make us weak, Next morning they fed us rice with worms in it. We ate them. My friend Fidel Vela from Rio Grande City (Loya was from San Benito, Texas) said he wasn't going to make it. In the morning he was dead.

"There were 100 to 150 bodies a day. We dug shallow holes and covered the bodies with mud. Finally we reached Camp O'Donnell on my 20th birthday. We had walked eighty miles. People kept dying.

"It was even worse after we were crowded into prison ships. At sea we heard concussions like depth charges. Every time there was a threat from our submarines, we would catch it. They beat us and made us kneel on the hot steel deck. Our knees were blistered. They took the sick guys below. We never saw them again. We didn't have water and drank our own urine. We kept throwing bodies overboard. I don't know how long the trip took. We lost track of time."

In Japan he was put to work loading ships. A load of timber shifted, crushing his foot.

"They gave me a rag and a stick and told me to fix it myself."

He still walks with a painful limp. He also suffered from dysentery and malaria.

"One officer could read Japanese. He told us to keep scraps of paper. In this way we learned we were winning the war. Our (American) doctor told those of us with broken bones to hit them to make them swell so we wouldn't have to work.

"Then they started treating us better. We could see B-29s bombing across the bay and knew it would soon be over. P-51s strafed a little refinery near us. Tanks caught fire, but a plane turned our way with machine guns blazing. Some of our people—American, British, and Dutch—were hit. A sergeant friend lost his leg.

"Our regular guards left, and we were afraid we might be killed after going through so much. Then it was over and they dropped us food. We made an American flag out of the parachutes. I wouldn't fly home. Not after all that. I came by boat. We were free.

"It's hard for people today to believe this happened. I am a Christian. I don't like the Japanese, but I have learned to forgive them. It was war. They were mean. They did it to destroy us. It wasn't just something in history books. It happened.

"I might be brainwashing my kids. I tell them to love this country and fight for it. No other country is like it. You can't really appreciate freedom until you lose it. Respect that flag and defend it if you must. If I had to, I'd do it again."

(April 6/April 9, 1979)

'This guard helped us. He was O.K.'

"When you tell about it, it sounds like Hogan's Heroes," Col. B. J. Martin said of his years in a Japanese prisoner-of-war camp. "It wasn't like that at all."

But you wouldn't know it if you heard him and his old comrade, British Brigadier E. J. Curran, CBE. The mind remembers the pleasant and buries the horrors of the past. So the two old soldiers giggled, chortled, and slapped their knees with laughter recalling the lighter moments of their great adventure that started in 1942.

"I named him Old Cock," Martin said, "because he was so feisty and would fight anybody or anything. He wasn't going to shave. That was against regulations. The men took him down and shaved him."

"By God, they did, the American lads," Curran said ruefully. "Never mind, it was coming in all black and white anyway."

The brigadier was captured when Hong Kong fell and was in several prisons before he was shipped to Tokyo and the camp holding the Americans.

"The Japs considered me an undesirable," he laughed.

"I was going to run the ship aground on the China coast. I had the Jap machine gunners all located so I could finish them off. I turned to a naval officer and told him to run the ship aground.

" 'I can't do that. I'm a torpedo officer. I know nothing about a ship's machinery,' he said. There went my plan. Tell him, B. J., how we were going to steal the plane and fly out of Japan."

"We located the plane and had it all worked out," Martin said. "When our work truck passed the plane, we realized the crew was sleeping under it and there was an armed guard."

"Just as well," Curran said. "He'd never flown a plane in his life."

"I figured if we could get the plane up, there'd be no trouble getting it down," Martin said.

"That part of the plan worried me," the brigadier said.

"We did the work of coolies. Our camp was in the rail terminal. We held school in smuggling food into the camp. If they were caught, the Japs beat the devil out of them. Each man kept 60 percent, and 40 percent went into a pool to feed sick and undernourished prisoners," Martin said.

"We waited until serving time to cook. We cooked in the overhead, under the floor, in the walls. So much cooking was going on the lights nearly went out in the commandant's office," Curran said. "Some of your Navy chaps learned how to tap a power line with a needle. One guard insisted that we bow to him. B. J. lined up 250 men behind him, and he bowed to every one of them. He never told us to do that again. Say, we taught men how to pinch pockets, eh, B. J.?"

They both laughed about picking pockets of Japanese during the confusion of air raids. "Pinched a Japanese dictionary once and we listened to Jap radio."

The prison was in metal buildings, a fact that saved the prisoners when Tokyo was destroyed by fire bombings. "It was a fire storm, not just a fire," Martin said.

"We pumped water on the roof with hand pumps until we were exhausted," the brigadier said. "You could put your arm out the door and it would burn. That's how hot it was."

"And B. J. got word to the Red Cross that we needed boots. Here came a B-29 flying low and dropped two tons of boots right through the roof," Curran said.

Martin, captured on Bataan, was almost beaten to death by prison guards. They showed me a photo of the guards and identified them by nickname.

"This one was executed. These five got thirty years. I went out and got this son-of-a-bitch and drug him back. This one helped us. He was O.K.," Martin said.

The two friends parted in Tokyo in 1945. Curran was named Commander of the British Empire by the Queen, an honor second only to knighthood.

A long line of British heroes waited to be honored by the Queen. She was busy for hours. "The Lord Chamberlain said, 'Don't kneel or you could be knighted,'" Curran laughed.

The brigadier is spending a fortnight with Martin. That ought to be almost enough time for them to relive the whole four years of prison life. It's a lot more fun this time around.

(June 12, 1979)

It's a good time to remember all those who made it in Japanese captivity . . .

After nearly four years of brutal captivity, the war was over. The Americans and others had been starved, beaten, worked as slaves, and humiliated by their Japanese captors. They had heard that the Japanese emperor had ordered a surrender. Now they could hear the drone of approaching American aircraft.

The men, weak from hunger and many on the verge of death from disease, cheered as the planes circled and leveled off for a bombing run. Only this time they were dropping drums filled with canned meats, cigarettes, medicines, candy, and clothing to the prison camp at Tinsen, Formosa.

The prisoners, many so wasted away they appeared almost skeleton-like, wet their lips in anticipation of the treat to which they had looked forward so long—the taste of freedom. Many had survived the Bataan Death March, years in one prison or another, then the sinking of a Japanese ship, which killed many of their companions. Red and white parachutes popped open. Two chutes failed to open, and the heavy drums crashed through the roof of the barracks, killing a number of the prisoners and injuring even more. After all their fortitude they were killed by countrymen seeking to help them. The same thing had happened to thousands of others who were killed in Japanese ships sunk by American bombers or submarines.

Manny Lawson, an Army officer, recounts his experiences and those of others who survived the most sadistic and brutal treatment ever received by American prisoners of war in a book entitled *Some Survived. An Epic Account of Japanese Captivity During World War II.*

He graphically describes the pain of dry beriberi, a disease brought on by lack of thiamine in the diet. It was a torture for many prisoners. The victims would lie with their feet in the air. The slightest touch brought terrible pain. He himself had wet beriberi, a disease that causes the body to hold vast amounts of water. He measured his water intake until they were fed soybeans and he began to return to normal. But a fellow prisoner drank and drank water until he literally exploded.

The Bataan Death March was terrible, but it was not as bad as other events in the years to come. Toward the end of the war, Lawton and 1,600 others were sent to Japan. Only 400 reached there alive.

The survival of a group of seventy-five who were on a ship sunk by our planes was remarkable. Hundreds were killed aboard the ship where hundreds of others had died of dehydration. They were thrown into fifteen-foot seas in the wake of a typhoon. Many were machine-gunned in the water by a Japanese cruiser. Others clung to bits of debris and reached safety. One group played dead in a lifeboat, and a Japanese destroyer held its fire. Miraculously, a box containing sails for the boat and the mast floated to them, and they sailed to safety.

Lawton captures the true horror of the camps and how military men were transformed into animals whose only concern was survival. One friend for whom he had given food earlier refused to help him when he was near death. Yet another man, a wheeler-dealer in black-market food, accepted a check on his hometown bank and sold him tins of meat that saved his life.

May 30 seems like Memorial Day to me, and it's a good time to remember all those who made it in Japanese captivity and all those who didn't. They deserve more than a passing thought.

(May 30, 1985)

No Peace in the Pacific

Photo by the author

Pearl Harbor's Bowfin Park Waterfront Memorial pays silent tribute to the fifty-two U.S. submarines and the more than 3,500 men of the 'Silent Service' who were lost in World War II. The *Bowfin* is restored as a tribute to all the submariners of WW II and to all of the members of the U.S. Submarine Force, both past and present.

Christmas 1941 was not a very happy time for Rear Adm. W. L. "Bull" Wright, USN, (Ret.). His submarine, the *Sturgeon*, entered Manila Bay that day.

"The harbor was filled with sunken and sinking ships. The docks were wrecks and the city was on fire. That day Gen. Douglas MacArthur declared Manila an open city and all military personnel were removed. It was not a very Merry Christmas," he recalled.

We sat in the parlor of his Aransas Pass, Texas, home where he has lived since his retirement in 1946. It is crowded with a comfortable clutter. Mementos of a life at sea and by the sea fill nearly every inch of wall space: a gooney bird skull, a sextant, and a ring from the compass of a sunken Japanese cruiser.

The twin dolphins on the mantel announce the residence of a submariner. And a framed skull and crossbones flag with eight torpedoes on it announce some of his record. There are certificates announcing his Legion of Merit from the Army for evacuating soldiers from Corregidor before that fortress fell, the Bronze Star, Silver Star, and the Navy Cross with a star in lieu of a second Navy Cross for bravery in sinking Japanese shipping.

He admits to one error he made as commander of submarine forces. He felt the subdued lighting on the subs could be improved. He ordered fluorescent lights installed. Later a sub commander stormed into his office and demanded to know what stupid individual had replaced the old lights. That's when he learned that the first depth charge attack caused all of the fluorescent bulbs to explode.

"I confessed I was the culprit," the admiral said.

He estimates more than 500 depth charges have exploded in his immediate vicinity. He spun story after story about torpedo attacks and depth charge attacks until I could almost hear the deafening clang of the explosion and the shattering of dishes and glassware.

"I hated destroyers," he said. "There was this one in particular, an old World War I four-stacker named *Kamikaze*. When I was in charge of operations, I gave specific orders for that destroyer to be sunk. Every sub recorded its speed as thirty-two knots. The captain kept that old destroyer moving fast. I don't know who that captain was, but I'll have to hand it to him. His ship was one of the few combat ships afloat in the Japanese Navy when the war was over."

Off Borneo his torpedo officer, Chester W. Nimitz Jr., reported a row of Japanese destroyers.

"'No,' I said, 'that's debris.' About then shells landed all around us. We dived and finally got away from their depth charge attack.

"'Say, Captain, that was pretty active debris,' young Nimitz said.

"Ever hear of bulkheading? It's a Navy word that has no equivalent—when two people talk so a third will hear them. One sailor said to another, 'The Old Man's all right, but I think his eyes are going.'"

Fleet Commander Chester Nimitz brought a Honolulu newspaper with the headline "Sub Sinks Jap Carrier" to Mrs. Wright and said, "That one is ours." It later turned out to be an aircraft ferry and not a carrier but a big ship nonetheless.

In those days the sub was isolated for months at a time. Now there is instant communication. "They can get a decision in seconds. What I fear is that officers aren't getting the experience of making decisions and won't be making them if a time comes they are required to," Wright said.

He and others knew they had to make decisions when Pearl Harbor was attacked and they realized no help was coming. "My orders were to stand off Singapore and repair to a friendly port to the south in the event we were out of torpedoes, food, or fuel—only the friendly ports to the south kept disappearing."

He got fuel from the Dutch in Java before that island fell. He made his way to Australia with a load of wounded soldiers and prepared to take the war to Japan.

"After the war was over, I came down with a bad case of malaria and a stomach ailment," he said. "So I was medically discharged.

"Now it all doesn't seem to mean much. People scarcely notice Pearl Harbor Day. I think we need a little more flag waving and hooraying in this country."

When he and his wife celebrated their 50th wedding anniversary, in 1976, his former crew members elected one of their number to attend the festivities. He flew in from California, spent an hour at the party, and flew out.

"That was something," the admiral said.

He doesn't think much of the bureaucracy but thinks people are shortsighted when they deride "the military mind." He remembered again the losses in World War II because of unpreparedness.

"It is the duty of the professional to know what is needed to defend this country and then try to convince people who furnish the money. The claim of economy can be false."

And the admiral does his part. He raises the flag every day in his front yard and doesn't remember that miserable Christmas so many years ago.

(December 13/December 14, 1977)

He gave his life
helping his friends.

'E carried me away
To where a dooli lay
An' a bullet come and drilled the beggar clean
'E put me safe inside
An' just before he died,
'I 'ope you liked your drink,' sez Gunga Din . . .

Wallace L. Dinn Jr. of Corpus Christi was no water boy, but his comrades called him Gunga Dinn. And he gave his life helping his friends. On January 5, 1943, he was escorting heavy bombers in the Guadalcanal area when he noticed fighter planes below under attack, outnumbered twenty to one. He went to their assistance and was shot down in flames. It was his fiftieth mission in less than three months.

It was early in the war, and Japan still ruled the air. Lt. Dinn had already been shot down twice. The first adventure sounds like a television scriptwriter's dream. The flight left Henderson Field on Guadalcanal to bomb the Japanese seaplane base at Rekata Bay. Dinn's P-38 was hit on a strafing run. The cockpit filled with smoke, but he managed to get the burning plane to 2,000 feet and bailed out.

He made his way to a native village and was welcomed when they learned he was American. He persuaded a young man named Eric and several others to paddle their boats toward Tulagi, 160 miles away. At another village he picked up a 20-foot war canoe and four paddlers. There were huge crocodiles on the beach.

"The natives told me two Japs had been in this locale several weeks before, but the crocs had eaten them before the natives could assist them back to Rekata Bay," he wrote in a letter to his father.

Natives told him of a Japanese pilot on a little island fifteen miles away. His Zero had been hit over Guadalcanal, but he had made it 140 miles before ditching.

Dinn instructed the natives to land on the island at breakfast when the pilot would put his pistol down to eat. It worked as planned. Natives grabbed the pilot and his pistol as Dinn walked into his camp.

"He demanded that I shoot him," Dinn wrote, "and seemed to think I was a weakling when I refused."

Later he felt sorry for his prisoner and gave him his last two cigarettes. The prisoner returned the favor the next day. He overturned the canoe, and they all had to swim for shore.

Dinn located a coast watcher, but his radio was out of order. The canoe trip continued. As they prepared for a sixty-mile voyage in open seas, he received word a British boat was across the island. They hiked over a 2,000-foot mountain range and paddled five miles to reach it. During the march the prisoner refused to move, but natives persuaded him with a rusty bayonet. The trip covered eight days and 120 miles. In all the boat recovered two Navy pilots, a gunner, and a Marine pilot who had been lost for twenty-eight days.

After a day's rest on Guadalcanal, Dinn was flying again. Weeks later he was forced down at sea. He swam his raft to an island, where a flying boat picked him up. Again he was in the air the next day. He was credited with sinking a Japanese warship in a dive-bombing attack off Guadalcanal before his last mission.

His commander, Col. John W. Mitchell, came to visit the elder Dinn when he returned to the States. He told him how his son died and presented the father with the pistol his son had taken from the Japanese pilot—the souvenir of a short but remarkable combat career.

Lt. Dinn was awarded the Distinguished Service Cross, the nation's second highest military honor. Plans to name an airfield for him never materialized.

> 'Though I've belted you and flayed you,
> By the livin' Gawd that made you,
> You're a better man than I am, Gunga Dinn.
> —Rudyard Kipling

(March 23, 1979)

He gave full credit for anything that was accomplished to his enlisted men.

During the early stages of World War II, America was desperately in need of heroes. Marines were hanging onto a precarious foothold on Guadalcanal. Japanese destroyers and cruisers came down "the Slot" from their base at Bougainville so often they earned the title "Tokyo Express." The Japanese were trying to reinforce and supply their troops and bombard the beachhead and Henderson Field.

The only thing that stood between them and this objective was eight 77-foot wooden boats powered by Packard marine engines, Patrol Torpedo Boats, known as "PTs" and later made famous by the story of young John F. Kennedy.

For four months men and their craft were pushed mercilessly night after night. They patrolled slowly in the darkness until they found a target. They fired their torpedoes, set off a smoke screen, and tried to outrun their pursuers. The PTs sank or damaged many ships. More importantly, they created confusion that made the Japanese tentative. The officers and men became among the heaviest decorated in the history of the Navy. Even before Kennedy they gave PT Boats a heroic image.

Among them were Lt. Robert L. Searles, Lt. Henry S. Taylor, Lt. Lester H. Gamble, Lt. (jg) James Brent Greene, Lt. John Malcom Searles, Lt. Hugh M. Robinson, Lt. Cmdr. Alan R. Montgomery, and Lt. (jg) Leonard A. (Nick) Nikoloric. Nikoloric was one of the few PT-ers who never talked of his experiences.

I had planned to try to get him to talk, but everyone said it wouldn't work. His wife, Mary, says he never spoke of the war. He died of cancer in July 1988. He was Phi Beta Kappa at Princeton and a graduate of the Yale School of Law. He was an adviser to President Lyndon Johnson and to Hubert Humphrey and the National League of Cities. There was no mention in the obituary of his war record.

Researching him, I find he was on the cover of *Life* magazine in May 1943, with Taylor and Robert Searles. He gave full credit for anything that was accomplished to his enlisted men. He insisted the *Life* story be told from their viewpoint.

The crew was involved in a number of skirmishes, in which they had a hand in sinking two destroyers and a submarine. Perhaps Nick's admiration for his men came from a torpedo attack when the Japanese found him before he found them. Suddenly PT 37 found itself in the blinding glare of searchlights from two destroyers, which opened fire.

A salvo of 4.7-inch shells straddled the boat, stunning all on deck. The boat was on collision course with the enemy. Torpedoman John Der came to, thought the explosion was a misfired torpedo, and banged the percussion cap, sending a torpedo into the midships of a Japanese destroyer.

John Legg, quartermaster, crawled into the cockpit, pushed the throttles up full and did a sharp turn as gunner Leon Nale crawled back into his turret and and knocked out both searchlights with his 50-caliber machine guns—an extraordinary accomplishment.

On the fantail a gunner named Crossen revived and opened the valve on the smoke-screen generator. As the officers recovered, they saw the end of a perfectly executed torpedo attack and withdrawal under the cover of a smokescreen. And not an order had been issued.

On November 13, 1942, when only five boats were operating, orders came to penetrate the destroyer screen and attack the Japanese fleet, a suicide mission. They approached a huge fleet in darkness, convinced they were on their last patrol. Then an American admiral radioed them to get out of the way. The fleet they had seen was ours.

Nikoloric and his crew jubilantly pulled over and had grandstand seats at the naval Battle of Guadalcanal.

Back home, he and other officers were placed on exhibit as heroes to sell war bonds—a very distasteful role to Nikoloric.

In the meantime his boat, PT 37, with new officers and men, was hit in the gas tanks and exploded. Only one man survived. It is small wonder that Nick Nikoloric did want to talk about heroics.

(November 21, 1988)

'Nobody knew he was going to be president, so the crew's respect was earned.'

As the anniversary of the death of President John F. Kennedy approaches, there will be many stories and books about his life, some critical and some laudatory. Such books inspired William F. Liebenow to write an article for the *PT Boater*, a publication for former PT sailors. Liebenow was the skipper of PT 157 on the patrol during which Kennedy's PT 109 was sliced in two by the Japanese destroyer *Amagiri*. His boat later rescued Kennedy and ten other survivors.

Liebenow wrote, "My criticism of most books ... has been that the writers ... were not PT Boat sailors, they were not at the scene at that time, and ... they were nitpickers and sensation hunters trying to find flaws in his military ability to prove him as unfit president; or they went the other way and tried to build up a couple of incidents involving war action against the enemy into extraordinary feats which qualified him to be a world leader ...

"... Kennedy was no more or no less than any other PT Boat sailor. To my knowledge he never claimed to be. He was given the Navy and Marine Corps Medal for saving the life of crewman Patrick McMahon after PT 109 was sunk. I have never heard or read anything that suggests he was not entitled to this medal. JFK was respected and liked by his crew. Nobody knew that he was going to be president, so the crew's respect was earned. People liked him because he was likeable, even if he did talk with that Boston-Harvard accent."

Arguments concerning Kennedy as a boat skipper center around the incident when his boat was rammed the night of August 1-2, 1943, during action north of New Georgia Island in the South Pacific. The Japanese were making a last effort to shell Americans and supply their own trapped troops.

The raid started in confusion, for at dusk on August 1 eighteen Japanese bombers attacked the PT base at Lumbari Island, hitting two boats. A bomb launched torpedoes from PT 164, and they raced erratically around the bay until they beached, causing no damage.

Liebenow said four boats went on the patrol that night. The lead pair met a line of destroyers. They fired torpedoes, which missed, and the tubes on the 109 caught fire, illuminating the area for enemy gunners.

Only one boat was equipped with radar. It fired its torpedoes and retreated to base, leaving the other boats in the dark. They had no contact with one another, and each was attempting to attack independently, resulting in what Capt. Robert J. Bulkeley Jr. called "the most confused and least effective action in the Solomon Island campaign."

Perhaps another action two weeks before, when American B-25 bombers attacked PTs and destroyed two with the loss of one plane when the boats returned fire, was even more confused, but that was an all-American brawl.

On the August 1 patrol the second two boats became separated in the darkness. Naval gunfire appeared to be from shore batteries. For this the tactic was to lie low until discovered.

A ship came out of the darkness. The Japanese captain ordered a hard port turn. He got a hard starboard turn. The bow of the destroyer knifed through the gasoline tanks of the 80-foot PT Boat. It exploded with a flash. Two men died. Kennedy had operated his boat on one engine to avoid showing a white wake, but he was without instant mobility. Likely he could not have avoided the collision even with all three engines running, and his boat was too close to the ship to use its torpedoes. The destroyer never slowed. It disappeared in the darkness. Later it would be hampered by damaged propellers bent by the PT's wreckage.

Ten miles away the other boats assumed a PT had made a torpedo hit. They returned to base and did not miss the 109 until morning.

Briefly there was a fire, but the force of the speeding destroyer had pulled thousands of gallons of high-octane fuel away from the boat. The aft half of the boat sank. The bow floated. Kennedy and another officer swam out and rescued four crewmen, some of whom were badly burned. Kennedy suffered an injured back, a condition that would bother him the rest of his life. As the wreckage began to sink, they towed the men four miles against a strong current to a small island. There were eleven survivors.

Kennedy swam out to a point where other boats might pass. None came. In returning he was carried two miles off course by currents. They swam to another small island, hailed natives in a canoe, and convinced them they were not hostile. Kennedy carved a message on a coconut husk, the natives carried it to a coast watcher, and Liebenow's boat was dispatched to the rescue. The rescue was a routine mission, Liebenow said. Success was celebrated with medicinal alcohol provided by a pharmacist's mate.

Liebenow asked Kennedy how the 109 was sunk.

"Lieb, to tell the truth, I don't know," Kennedy said.

During the 1960 presidential campaign Kennedy said, "Lieb, if I get all the votes from the people who claim to have been on your boat the night of the pickup, I'll win easily."

(I've heard it said PT 109 would have had ten decks and four elevators to accommodate all the people who later claimed they served aboard it.)

Lon C. Hill III, a PT commander in the Mediterranean and later in the Pacific, said Kennedy invited former PT officers to the White House. They presented him with a carved glass trophy as the most successful PT alumnus. Kennedy apologized to his fellow officers about the heroic way the movie *PT 109* portrayed him. He was well aware of the fouled-up mission and didn't want them to think he was by any means claiming to be a hero, Hill said.

You would never convince members of his crew who were saved because Kennedy risked his life for them that he was no hero.

Liebenow concludes that the sinking of the 109 will grow into a semi-legend on the order of George Washington and the cherry tree.

"As with the cherry tree, it was not the incident," he wrote, "but what the man did afterwards that swelled it to historical importance."

(August 28, 1981/November 15, 1988)

Carr died
as he was pulled away
from his gun.

A guided missile frigate that will be launched at Seattle on January 6 will be named the USS *Paul Henry Carr*. Carr was a twenty-year-old Oklahoma farm boy who died a hero aboard the destroyer escort *Samuel B. Roberts* in the Battle of Leyte Gulf on October 25, 1944.

All the hurt, shock, pain, and pride of the loss have returned to Mrs. Lucille Seifert. Carr was her brother, the only boy among eight sisters.

"I only wish our dad were alive," she said. "He was so proud of Paul Henry."

The family farmed near Checotah, Oklahoma. "He was a year older than me. He blacked my eye and I blacked his when we were kids. I tagged along everywhere he went. They said he was a born leader. He was good at getting other people to do his chores," she smiled.

"He was the second-best center in Oklahoma his senior year, and if there had been no war, he would have had a good chance to go to college on a football scholarship. He joined the Navy in May 1943. He came home on leave before his ship was launched in Houston early in 1944."

The *Samuel B. Roberts* was named for a young sailor who died piloting a landing craft to rescue Marines stranded on a beach in 1942. The "*Sammy B*" was with two other DEs, three destroyers, and five jeep carriers under the command of Rear Adm. Clifton A. Sprague off Samar Island when a column of Japanese battleships led by destroyers and heavy cruisers appeared.

The outgunned destroyers and escorts attacked. There was smoke and confusion. The *Sammy B*. maneuvered within 4,000 yards of a cruiser before it was discovered. It fired three torpedoes. Two struck the enemy ship. During this time the after 5-inch gun fired as fast as it could have been fired. During the battle it fired 300 rounds. But soon Japanese 5-inch, 8-inch, and 14-inch shells began making hits.

One exploded in the lower handling room. The main steam line was ruptured. The after deckhouse was blown away. A 14-inch shell opened a hole ten feet high and forty feet long on the portside. The No. 2 engine room was wiped out. The ship was shot to pieces.

Without power, gun captain Paul Henry Carr and his crew hand loaded, rammed, and fired six more shells. The gun had made forty hits on an enemy cruiser. The powder charge on the seventh try exploded with the breech open, killing all the gun crew but three. Only one would survive.

As the crew abandoned ship, a petty officer checked the mount and found Carr trying to push a 54-pound shell in the wrecked loading tray. His intestines were blown away. He took the shell from Carr and removed the wounded man. He returned to find the dying sailor again trying to load the last shell. Carr died as he was pulled away from his gun.

Eighty-nine men died, but 128 survived. A Japanese destroyer came by and filmed the men in the water but made no effort to strafe or mangle them with the ship's screws.

Crewmen are trying to find other survivors to attend the launching to honor their dead shipmate. Another frigate has already been named for the skipper of the *Samuel Roberts*, the late Robert W. Copeland, who retired a rear admiral.

Mrs. Seifert proudly shows the Silver Star certificate signed by President Franklin D. Roosevelt and the citation by Secretary of the Navy James Forrestal. She shows his Purple Heart and Victory Medal.

"I feel sad all over again," she said with emotion. "But I feel proud, too. It's a feeling I can't describe."

She'll be prouder yet when the *Carr* hits the water.

(May 11, 1982)

'I have decided to tell the men to fight to the last breath.'

The bombing and shelling had been going on for days. Many of the defenders were dead or wounded. Buildings were destroyed and the men were hungry. Big bombers filled the skies, and carrier planes strafed and bombed the huddled survivors. They swore they would fight to the death.

There aren't many such accounts of the Japanese view of the American fleet in the South Pacific as it sent in shells and disgorged hundreds of landing craft. Auctioneers Clay and Irene Moore found among items to be auctioned an envelope containing a typewritten translation of a diary kept by a Japanese lieutenant commander identified only as Ex. O. The envelope also contained ten snapshots of the bodies of Japanese soldiers, possibly including that of the author, all horribly mangled by fire and explosives.

The first dates are November 17 and 18, 1943. The location is likely one of the lesser islands in the Gilbert chain. The main target there was Tarawa, where Marine casualties were more than 3,000.

"Big bombers came over and dropped a few bombs for the sixteenth time. A few AA guns fired at the planes. Our patrol boat reports they will be ready for the planes or any invasion. Two of our radars are out of order.

"Nov. 20. Thirty-two planes from the aircraft carrier raided this place. Eight big bombers and sixteen small planes dropped numerous bombs ... Naval guns from battleships ... did a lot of damage. Thirteen ships have been sighted. Nineteen of our officers have withdrawn to some unknown place.

"Nov. 21. We haven't eaten since yesterday, 0400. We have sighted two battleships, four cruisers and other naval craft. All ships opened fire on us. Enemy planes have bombed and strafed us from the east and west. Most of the coconut trees have been destroyed ... Enemy tanks have landed ... Their troops followed behind the tanks when leaving the landing crafts. Our commanding officer told the men to defend the island to the last man ...

"Nov. 22 and 23. We haven't eaten for three days, except for coconuts. We had another big battle tonight and a lot of men have been killed and wounded ... While moving the wounded, we came in contact with enemy tanks. After the tanks opened fire on us, our commander told the men to disperse and withdraw.

"Nov. 24. Our commander hasn't any idea of the number of casualties we suffered. It was reported a lot of enemy trucks, tanks and small vehicles have landed. Lucky we have a lot of small lakes to obstruct their passage. Today I don't know whether I will live or not, and I have decided to tell the men to fight to the last breath. I asked for volunteers to hold the lines even with their lives. Many have responded."

There were more battles and casualties. By December 4 his group had only seven men left.

"Dec. 7 ... Two tanks from the sea came back. Five of our men hid in the water near the beach. We saw the American troops eating nearby. We worried as to how we could escape. We decided to swim away. We swam for sixty or seventy meters. When we came out of the water, the skin on our hands and face looked like dead men's skin.

"Dec. 8. Today is the second anniversary of our great Asiatic and South Seas campaign. We have been thinking about our glorious past campaigns. We did not see the enemy, so we went to look for water. We made up our minds to fight to the end, or to commit suicide if we are to be captured.

"Dec. 11. Today looks like another clear day. I feel like singing a song. I hope the tanks won't come today so I can rest my body.

"Dec. 12. As usual we had coconuts for breakfast. We saw three boats headed for Butaritari from Kuma Village. We plan to depart from Kuma Village on the 13th or 14th.

"Dec. 13. This morning I decided to go back and gather up the rest of my personal belongings and go somewhere else. At midnight I washed my head and face."

There were no further entries. The Japanese officer's luck apparently had run out.

(June 23, 1988)

He found a wing
with a white star
in a faded blue circle.

He told a lie, which fate turned to truth, which made Joe Wright a hero instead of a goat. He had permission for a week's vacation from his Air Force bomb group on Guam. It turned out to be a three-week odyssey, which Wright, now a Presbyterian minister at Refugio and Tivoli, considers the adventure of his life.

"My brother-in-law was teaching school on the island of Majuro in the Marshall Islands. My friend, Sam Sasser, was a missionary there. Sam was waiting for me. His students had left that day aboard a copra trading ship and were at Arno Atoll seventy miles away. He asked if I wanted to go. I didn't know what I was getting into. We watched the waves and jumped the reef in a fourteen-foot boat and nearly swamped. We ran into a tropical storm and it looked like the end. We found land and jumped another reef in heavy seas and reached the ship. It was the *Meico Queen*, a rusty tub that would have been a fit companion to the *African Queen*.

"The people of Mili Atoll were untouched by civilization, even though their island was littered with the wreckage of World War II. Natives had seen very few white men. They were happy to see men of God. The reception was awesome. They literally buried us with leis and set about preparing a feast, roast pig and all."

After several sermons the natives led him on a tour of the island. Jungle growth had reclaimed a landing strip the Japanese had installed, and the island was pockmarked with bomb craters. Wreckage of Japanese warplanes was everywhere. In the undergrowth he found a wing with a white star in a faded blue circle. Sasser found an instrument panel with a radio call number on it. Native boys told the story their parents told of the wreckage.

"In late 1943 and early 1944 the airfield at Mili was strafed by a lone American fighter plane. The pilot not only made low strafing runs against fortifications but actually landed, taxied about firing machine guns and cannons at targets around the strip, then took off before gunners could take aim.

"A doctor on Majuro said he saw it as a boy of fourteen. Each time the plane landed, it wreaked havoc on Mili airfield. Finally gunners set up an ambush and caught the pilot in a crossfire, knocking him down in the jungle."

He was pulled from the wreckage and forced to run a gauntlet where he was beaten with clubs. A Japanese officer beheaded him with his sword after troops made bets about how far a headless man could run.

Wright located the records with the radio number and learned the pilot was Capt. Clifford Erdman of California. He was based on Makin Island 350 miles from Mili and was last seen on a strafing run while escorting bombers. The tail flew off his P-39, which crashed in the jungle. Erdman was listed as missing in action. The Air Corps had no record of the captain's role on the Japanese runway.

Wright sent a radio message to his Air Force commanding officer on Guam saying the boat had engine trouble and he would be late. At sea the boat's engine did quit, leaving seasick natives, pigs and chickens, plus a cargo of smelly dried coconut adrift. The captain asked him to find out where they were. He charted a location with an antique sextant and another trade ship came to their aid. The captain wrote a letter of appreciation so he wouldn't get in trouble. But he was not in trouble. In fact, the Air Force gave him a letter of commendation for helping the islanders.

The ship's captain also told him how to find where Amelia Earhart crashed. Speculation about the famous woman pilot continues forty-two years after she and her co-pilot, Fred Noonan, disappeared on their globe-circling attempt. How and where did Earhart die? Was she an early-day U-2 type spy? Or was she a victim of her own carelessness or inadequate equipment?

The Earhart legend, considerable since she was the object of a full-time publicity campaign by her husband, G. P. Putnam Jr., has grown steadily since her death. She was a pioneer woman pilot with many firsts to her credit and a pioneer for women's rights.

Some authorities believe her plane crashed and sank not far from Howland Island as she attempted a 2,500-mile flight from Lae, New Guinea, on July 2, 1937. Her last radio message indicated she was lost and running low on fuel. No physical evidence as to her fate has ever been found.

But Wright, after his experience in 1967, is satisfied she did not crash at sea. "The captain of the copra trading ship *Meico Queen* had never known of a white man and woman crashing in the area. But he showed me an old man on Enajet Island (in Mili Atoll) who knew something. Sam Sasser served as interpreter. The old man remembered a plane falling in the lagoon at low tide. He calculated the year by remembering weddings, deaths, births, and storms. He said it was thirty years ago (or 1937). Remember, this man did not speak English, did not read newspapers, or listen to the radio. He knew nothing of history or Amelia Earhart.

"He remembered well because a woman was flying the machine. 'She was dressed like a man and wore her hair short like a man,' the old Marshall Islander said. The woman was tall and slender. The man was also slender. He had a white towel on his head. Apparently he suffered a head injury and had been bandaged.

" 'We did not get too curious,' the man said. 'The Japanese were hard. One woman disobeyed and they cut her head off. In a couple of days the Japanese came and took the man and woman away. They took the flying machine away, too.'

"He said the woman hid some papers in the hollow of a tree. I was tempted to go out and look at every tree on the island, but that was thirty years before and the jungle was thick," Wright said.

Earlier Wright had read Fred Goerner's book *The Search for Amelia Earhart*, which included interviews with various natives of Saipan. A number reported a white man and woman had been held prisoner on that island before World War II. One woman told of giving the woman prisoner fruit. Shown pictures of Amelia Earhart, she said the prisoner fit the description but was older and sick. The woman died of dysentery, she had heard. Then the man was executed. Both were buried in an unmarked grave.

Author Goerner became so excited over Rev. Wright's interview he wanted to make another trip to the South Pacific. Another author, Dick Strippel, was so drawn by Wright's information he began research and wrote his own book, *Amelia Earhart, the myth and the reality*.

Goerner's book hints darkly that conspiracies have locked up the Earhart secret in military archives all these years. Strippel doesn't think so. The spy theory started after the U-2 affair, he said. He believes she died at sea because of poor communications and there is nothing to hide. South Sea Islanders, he says, are so anxious to please they change questions into answers, telling the interviewer what he wants to hear. He's going to have to go a long way to convince Rev. Wright. Wright went a long way to uncover his secret.

(July 19/July 20, 1979)

Thorpe didn't think the Lido Road . . . was worth the sacrifice . . .

He had his share of successes, but he remembers mostly the disappointments. He's a big man, erect at seventy. He plopped down the notebook. Typewritten single-spaced, it is the story of his life.

Here is how E. D. Thorpe summed it up: "Most people say I should write a book. Maybe that's why I'm doing this. I have had some unusual experiences. But as I've always said, romance and adventure are just dirty, hard, and dangerous work while it's going on. It's just in retrospect that there appears to be any glamour in it. Certainly I've found myself hanging on to the dirty end of the stick most of my life."

The writing is rough, as if he had taken a recording while he told stories at a table at the corner tavern. But the meat is there. Had he the technical ability, it might have been a powerful autobiography. It is written almost as an act of defiance—a taunt at life that has always knocked him down, no matter how much effort he was expending to get ahead.

Thorpe is bitter. He worked so hard and never reached the goals he set for himself. But he's alive, and that's something, if you happen to have been one of the survivors of Merrill's Marauders in Gen. "Vinegar Joe" Stilwell's Burma theater of action in World War II. They told Thorpe they were putting him in for the Silver Star for valor, but no one ever sent in the papers. They waited until right before his discharge to award him his Combat Infantry Badge, which would have entitled him to extra pay.

His father was a lazy ne'er-do-well. He loved his mother even though she burned his thumbs with matches to break him from sucking his thumb as a child. He learned to read early, made few friends in school, and was beaten up by other kids. At home he was whipped, but his brothers went unpunished for the same offenses.

He ran away from home at seventeen to Texas, then to California where he worked at dozens of jobs in the fields, in factories—wherever there was work—and bummed around the country. He captures the Depression era well and does the same with the peacetime Army he joined in 1939. But it is his account of the war in Burma that caught my attention.

Suffering from malaria, dysentery, lice, leeches, bad water, constant rain, jungle rot, and heat, and forced to carry heavy loads through jungles, across rivers, over mountains to face a superior Japanese force, the troops opened the Burma Road to China. They hoped for relief when they were pulled back, but they were sent back to even more privations. Sickness, fever, and wounds bought no exemptions. These were the men, commanded by Brig. Gen. Frank Merrill, who made a torturous 100-mile forced march to cut off the only Japanese supply line into the Hukawng Valley.

The survivors of that march were specters of their former selves, gaunt, hollow-eyed, and sick—more dead than alive. They were widely acclaimed as heroes. But Thorpe didn't think the Lido Road to China was worth the sacrifice, since the airlift had already eased the emergency.

"Outside of building General Stilwell's hurt ego, we didn't do a damn thing. I hope he rots in hell along with all the other egotistical bastards," he wrote.

He returned to the States and was immediately dressed down by a new lieutenant for not wearing a tie.

After the war he worked in a Kellogg's factory until he retired. He had a couple of unsuccessful marriages, learned to fly, and attended law school for a time. He moved to Texas to escape the snow in Michigan and to be near his grandchildren. His daughter divorced and her husband got custody of her children.

"Now that I've written this," he concluded, "I don't know whether anyone will ever read it or not. I wanted my grandchildren and great-grandchildren to know why I did things I did and what made me the way I am."

Someday I think those descendants would be proud to read E. D. Thorpe's account of his life.

(*June 12, 1987*)

'... I was that Marine ... who yelled at you guys.'

Winston "Wink" Shook can tell you about being caught between a rock and a hard place. The rock in this case was the island of Iwo Jima. The hard place would have been the Pacific Ocean—the alternate choice of a place to ditch a badly damaged B-29 bomber—where the crew members would be mere specks on the vast expanse of open sea.

The eight square miles of Iwo Jima are the most expensive real estate in the world. More than 5,000 U.S. Marines gave their lives to capture it in 1945 so that fighter planes could use it as a base to escort bombers from Saipan and Tinian in strikes over Japan. It would also serve as an emergency landing strip for B-29s.

Shook was a 17-year-old aerial gunner aboard a plane named *T Square 27*. The flight encountered heavy anti-aircraft fire in the fire-bomb attack. The plane was hit by an explosion that knocked out one engine and wounded two crewmen.

"It also knocked out our transfer pumps so that we were unable to transfer fuel to the main tanks. There was no way we could make it back to our base. Our pilot put it to a vote. Did we want to ditch at sea? Or did we want to land on Iwo? The island wasn't secured and fighting was still heavy there.

"There wasn't any question. We all voted for Iwo. If we ditched at sea, they'd probably never find us. Our pilot made a good landing on the Japanese airstrip. Before we landed, we could hear bullets going 'Whap!' on the sides of the plane. The Marines were dug in on one side of the runway and were shooting over us at the Japanese, who were shooting at us from Mount Suribachi.

"A Marine sergeant stood up in his foxhole and yelled, 'You guys had better get out of there and get in this hole or you're going to get your tails shot off!'

"Later they counted 1,900 bullet holes in our ship. They just rolled it over the cliff. I'd take a war in the air over that of the infantryman anytime. Funny thing. I was telling this story, and a fellow who used to work for Mobil Oil Co. here said, 'I know you are telling this right because I was that Marine staff sergeant who yelled at you guys.'

(The Marine was Don Farmer, after the war a crude-oil buyer for Mobil.)

"As soon as the airstrip was secured, they flew us back to our outfit. We, except for the two guys who were hit, were right back flying missions again."

The limit for missions was supposed to be thirty-five, but his crew made thirty-eight. "For some reason they didn't count that landing on Iwo as a mission," he said.

He has scrapbooks and mementos of his wartime experience. Among them are the leaflets in Japanese warning civilians in various cities that a bombing attack was coming up and that they should evacuate.

"Part of this was psychological warfare," he said.

Heat from the burning targets was intense. "Flak was heavy and our pilot thought he would take cover in a dark cloud. It was a thermal cloud the updraft sent us up 18,000 feet in no time. Then we were caught in a downdraft, and our co-pilot saved us and pulled out at about 1,000 feet."

The B-29 was a good plane, pressurized and much more comfortable than the smaller B-17 and B-24s. It was designed to fly up to 40,000 feet, but the generals said the targets were obscured, and for accuracy the big planes went in at about 7,000 feet, resulting in a much greater loss ratio. Japanese Zero fighter planes crashed into the bombers to bring many of them down.

"The first time our P-51s flew from Iwo, they caught the Japanese fighters by surprise and shot down ninety-seven of them. I saw one fighter get three of them on one pursuit swing. It was like a movie—planes exploding, crashing, smoking over the whole sky. It was like a movie scene."

The battle he had landed in the middle of had possibly saved his life in the skies over Japan, as U.S interceptor planes from Iwo Jima cleared out kamikazi planes that had been so deadly to the bombers.

(October 3, 1988)

Off Okinawa, the ship's luck seemed to be deserting her crew.

The Japanese kamikaze planes hadn't been paying much attention to smaller ships like destroyers. They were after the big stuff—troop transports, aircraft carriers, battleships, cruisers.

The suicide planes had been running the gauntlet for weeks. Ships and planes had raised a wall of fire, eliminating most of them. But every now and then one got through and caused heavy damage.

At dawn June 11, 1945, the USS *William D. Porter*, standing well off Okinawa on radar picket, spotted a single plane coming in out of the haze. General quarters sounded. Before gun crews could open up, the plane hit the radar mast and cartwheeled over the deck. A wing caught on the deck, swinging the fuselage over the side and under the ship, where its bomb exploded.

"I was going to my battle station in the wardroom," Dr. James L. Barnard recalls. "I was on the starboard side. The radar mast fell on the port side. The ship stopped and started to list. It had a big hole in the hull."

Water poured in. Boilers exploded.

The destroyer *William D. Porter* had been a lucky ship. Barnard went aboard her in the Aleutians.

"We were in the first fleet to bombard the Japanese mainland, the Kurile Islands. Five-inch shells from our guns hit, and we noticed tracer bullets rising in the air. Then we realized they had been bombed but never shelled. They were firing anti-aircraft guns into the air and not at us."

The *William D. Porter* dueled with two Japanese destroyers attempting to lead troop ships ashore back of Leyte Island in the Philippines.

"They didn't land any troops. We suffered some damage but didn't lose a man."

Then off Okinawa the ship's luck seemed to be deserting her crew. She was dead in the water. Other ships used submersible pumps. She couldn't push against the list. Her power was gone.

"They gave the abandon ship order and said, 'Doctor and wounded off first,'" Dr. Barnard said.

Because the bomb had exploded underwater, there were no shrapnel injuries. Some were burned and there were lesser injuries. Ten were hospitalized.

Dr. Barnard had been unpopular when he ordered the crew to take a first-aid course before they could get promoted. The training paid off when the ship was hit. Men trapped below were rescued and given first aid.

Sinking wouldn't seem to be the best of luck. But that same day a kamikaze plowed into another Fletcher Class destroyer. It hit the bridge and officers' and chiefs' quarters, killing every officer and all but one chief petty officer. A chief pharmacist mate was senior rank aboard.

Luck was in survival aboard Barnard's ship. The *William D. Porter* may have been the largest capital ship lost to enemy action without losing a man. All 320 men were removed before the ship turned over and sank.

"We were a close crew and have had three or four reunions. One officer, Bill Guy, was the first Democratic governor of North Dakota," Barnard said.

"Something else happened almost the same day we were sunk. Our daughter, Lynn, was born. The Navy public relations office made some play over that. They said I had been aboard for eighteen months. The censor made them change it to six months. He couldn't have known we were back in to San Francisco just nine months before."

Barnard got his survivor's leave and spent another year at the U.S. Naval Hospital in Corpus Christi before being discharged. The sinking was thirty-five years and eight children ago.

(June 10, 1980)

He lost sixty pounds and qualified as a cadet.

When Oscar Sherman Wyatt Jr., later a multi-millionaire Texas oilman, was a child, a neighbor described him as "a street fighter and a hard worker who would finish any job, even under a broiling sun." Years later, on the island of Okinawa, this would prove to be true.

Wyatt had always wanted to be a pilot. He and his friends built kites and dreamed of flying. When he was fourteen, they built a glider, tied it to the bumper of a car, and became airborne. At sixteen he took lessons and became a licensed pilot.

He was a lineman on the Navasota High School football team and played on the freshman team at Texas A&M. Known for his toughness and intimidating style, he was often penalized for holding. After Pearl Harbor he tried to enlist in the Army Air Corps, but the 240-pound weight that had helped him on the gridiron was far over the enlistment limit, 180 pounds.

Wyatt went on a strict diet, worked on two farms, exercised vigorously, and ran miles and miles. In a few months, he had lost sixty pounds and qualified as an Air Corps cadet.

He was assigned to a bomber squadron and flew combat missions in B-24s in the Pacific Theater. As the war was winding down, an engine failed, and his plane crashed on takeoff on Okinawa.

Although he suffered two broken legs and a fractured jaw and skull, he was able to crawl out and help his crew to safety. All survived.

(November 1, 2009)

'It was one of the few times ... everything went exactly as planned...'

Phil Ulrich wanted to talk about the last parachute jump of World War II.

"It was thirty-four years ago this week on the north end of Luzon," he said, spreading maps out over the table like it was the command post for an attacking army.

The maps, remarkedly detailed, were made up only on the day before the final attack was launched, on June 27, 1945, against the last 20,000 men in the Imperial Japanese Army who were on the island.

"Wasn't anything like the battle on Leyte. We went ashore by landing craft. No resistance. But the Japanese were ready inland, and one of the biggest ground battles in the Pacific cost us a lot of men."

But he was more interested in Luzon "because it was a picture-book invasion and the last parachute jump of the war." It also closed out the major fighting in the Philippines. The 511th Parachute Regiment landed at Camalaniugan Airfield. Japanese artillery was deployed to face an amphibious landing at Aparri to the north. The airborne and a column from the south tied up on schedule.

"It was one of the few times everything went exactly as planned, and everyone did exactly as they were supposed to do at exactly the right time—the fleet, artillery, support aircraft, the guerrillas, glider forces, parachute troops, everyone.

"At sundown Gen. (Robert) Bieghtler ordered a screen put up for a movie. It was Errol Flynn in *Mission Burma*. He was being the big hero with artillery exploding on the screen. All of a sudden Jap mortars opened up all around us. That was the most realistic war picture I ever saw."

Phil produced the secret battle orders, now yellow with age. They showed where "Gizzard Red Unit" he commanded was to land.

"I saved all this because it's a part of history," he said, "and for some reason more important to me than our actions in New Guinea, Leyte, and the occupation of Japan."

(June 29, 1981)

All four planes were hit by anti-aircraft fire on the bombing run.

It was only a small happening in the overall picture of a war, but it made a lasting impression on two local men. They are both insurance men with whom I have done business for many years. They have never met and only through a chance conversation did I put their stories together.

Some time ago State Farm Agent Pat Bednorz sent me a copy of *The Grey Geese Flyer*, a newsletter of the 11th Bomb Group Association. In it was a description of a bombing raid on Kure Naval Base in Japan on July 28, 1945, by B-24 bombers. Four of them, the *Moonlight Maid*, piloted by Lt. Dwight Cloud; the *Lonesome Lady*, piloted by Lt. Cartwright; the *Taloa*, piloted by Lt. Dubrinsky; and the flight leader, Lt. Turek, were in the third group over the target, the Japanese battleship *Haruna*. Each plane carried three 2,000-pound bombs. Jim Delaney, bombardier on the *Moonlight Maid*, wrote the account.

All four planes were hit by anti-aircraft fire on the bombing run. The *Lonesome Lady* was hit in the fuselage and burst into flames. All of the crew but the navigator bailed out safely. His body was never found. The *Taloa* received several direct hits and went into a steep glide. Five members of the crew parachuted. The pilot, Lt. Dubrinsky, was killed when his chute failed to open. Four men made it safely to the ground, but two were killed by angry civilians.

The *Moonlight Maid*, badly damaged, made it safely back to base, as did the plane piloted by Lt. Turek. Sgt. Abel, a gunner from the *Lonesome Lady*, was the first to bail out. He was captured separately and survived the war. Lt. Cartwright was taken to Tokyo for questioning and he presumably also survived.

The other survivors were taken to Chugoku Military Headquarters in Hiroshima where they joined other captured American airmen in prison. They all perished when the atom bomb was dropped on Hiroshima on August 6, 1945. Bednorz said, "While reading the story, some clicking went on in my brain. I thought, 'I saw this happen.' There were four planes in this flight of B-24s flying in our standard diamond formation and crossing about a 30-degree angle across our nose and some 200 feet below. I observed this with forward peripheral vision, since my gaze was glued on our own formation lead plane.

"We were in a very steep descent of some 1,000 feet a minute to escape the flak on our bomb run. Suddenly the four-plane formation was engulfed in a cloud of black smoke. I knew someone had been hit and perhaps the 2,000-pound bombs blew up. After a few microseconds only two planes emerged from the smoke. I was not in a position to observe any trace of the others."

Bednorz said his 42nd Squadron was credited with four or five hits on the battleship, which rolled on its side at the dock.

T. Frank Horner, semi-retired life insurance agent, mentioned B-24s and said he was a member of the same bomb group.

"We were supposed to have been on that same run," he recalls. "We were at the end of the runway preparing to take off when we were told our flight was canceled. Otherwise we would have been one of the four planes in that flight. Later we flew through a cloud of red brick dust from the A-bomb. We cheered because we knew it meant the war would be over. Then we learned the bomb had killed our men on the ground and there was no longer any joy in it."

T. Frank, the aerial gunner, and Pat, the pilot, have yet to meet personally. They will have a lot to talk over.

(February 4, 1988)

. . . the heroes were his buddies who didn't make it back.

It has been my privilege to know a real, honest-to-goodness hero. I've known him most of my life, yet I learned he was a hero only after he died. Melton Truax would not tell you he was a hero. He would be greatly embarrassed by all the pomp and circumstance in his name.

I don't think it was just modesty that wouldn't let Melton acknowledge the honors. To him, the heroes were his buddies who didn't make it back. He didn't want to diminish the contributions of those men. So he went quietly about his way, with his easy smile and friendly, even-tempered manner. Even his golf-playing friends knew nothing of his military record.

But he is dead now, too, and he is being honored at 2:30 p.m. August 6 by having the airfield at Corpus Christi Naval Air Station named Truax Field. Rear Adm. David R. Morris will be guest speaker at the dedication.

Melton would have nominated thirty-seven other pilots from Squadron 83 aboard the carrier *Essex*. They died as the Japanese furiously defended their homeland in 1945.

Melton came home with a hatful of medals but would never talk of them. In fact, he wouldn't tell you anything about his military career except the funny little things that happen to everyone who fights in a war.

He would never tell you about the two Navy Crosses, the Distinguished Flying Cross, the five Air Medals, the Bronze Star, a Presidential Citation, and all the others he picked up in a short period as an aviator aboard the USS *Essex*. After he was discharged, he declined to go to Jacksonville, Fla., to receive the medals with bands playing and the base personnel standing at attention.

He wouldn't let his wife, Virginia, put the ones she had so meticulously framed on display. He took them to his office and put them in a drawer until just before he retired a year ago.

"Why not let me put them up?" she asked. "After all, you are a hero."

"I am not a hero," he answered. "I'm just a guy who did my job like everyone else."

His idol was Lt. Cmdr. Dave Barry, his commanding officer, who was an ace many times over and was on his third tour of duty when he was killed in action May 13, 1945. The air group on the *Essex* lost half its pilots during that period.

Melton would be put out with us who nominated him for the honor. He was two years ahead of me at the Masonic Home and School in Fort Worth, Texas. Even there, he showed a brand of individualism that would make him an exceptional combat pilot who was to shoot down thirteen enemy planes in the air and destroy many more on the ground, among many exploits.

There was one cardinal rule at the Home. If you ran away, nobody came looking for you. You were history. You could not come back. In those Depression days there were more applications than there was space for children in the school. Melton's father had been dead only a year when his mother sent him there. He had a great attachment for his father and missed him dearly. He was nine years old. After three days he ran away.

Knowing he would head home, Bill Remmert, dean of boys, called his mother and asked her to bring him back. She did. Mr. Remmert talked to him at length and asked him to give the Home a chance. Two weeks later he was on the road again.

Mr. Remmert had taken a liking to him. Once more he broke the rule and had him sent back. This time he told Melton there were no more chances. Run away again, he would stay gone. Melton did stay. Until his dying day he was one of the strongest supporters of the Home and asked that any contributions in his memory be donated to it.

He also showed his independence in the Navy. Orders were that all pilots would stay below decks when the carrier was under attack by bombers or kamikaze planes. The skipper told them the government had too much tied up in their training to risk losing them. Their job was flying. But when a gun crew was knocked out, Melton could not restrain himself. He and another pilot took over the anti-aircraft station for the rest of the raid. The skipper did not get around to dressing them down until after the raid was over.

And off the coast of Japan, they were constantly being told each raid would be the last. It appeared that the war was about over, but anti-aircraft fire was still intense. The carrier was scheduled to return home as soon as hostilities ceased.

Melton grumbled he would not be able to say he had been in

Japan. So during a strafing raid over a major Japanese base, Japanese gunners were undoubtedly surprised to see a blue U.S. Navy Corsair make a touch-and-go landing during all the confusion. Melton had paid a visit to the Japanese mainland.

(Author's note: On a later occasion I mentioned this incident to a Navy admiral. "If I'd been his commanding officer and found out about that, he'd have been in a heap of trouble," the admiral laughed.)

After Melton's death his son, Frank, dug out the citations signed by Vice Adm. M. A. Mitscher, each beginning, "In the name of the President of the United States, the Commander, First Carrier Task Force, Pacific, presents . . ."

The first Navy Cross went to Ens. Myron Melton Truax "for distinguishing himself by extraordinary heroism in operations against the enemy while serving as a pilot in the vicinity of the Island of Okinawa on 27 March 1945. He sighted an enemy combatant ship and skillfully and courageously pressed an attack against it in the face of intense anti-aircraft fire. His strafing and rocket hits caused serious damage to the enemy vessel . . ."

The second Navy Cross—a medal ranking just below the Medal of Honor—was awarded for action off Okinawa May 4, 1945.

"During this fight he attacked a group of enemy aircraft, which was greatly superior in numbers, and in the action that followed, he shot down six of the enemy aircraft."

The Distinguished Flying Cross covered the period between March 19 and May 15 against Kyushu and Okinawa, where he "participated in twenty strikes and flights over enemy territory and inflicted extensive damage to enemy airfields and installations . . ."

The five Air Medals came from some fifty-five air strikes against the enemy, destroying installations and planes.

"He was proud of his military record," Virginia said. "He offered to go back during the Korean War when so many young, inexperienced pilots were being killed. But they wanted him to be an instructor. He didn't want it if it wasn't combat."

"All the pages in his flight log covering his combat record have been torn out," his son said.

As a kid Melton had a ready smile. That same flashing smile, brown eyes, and the rakish way he wore his Navy uniform made him a smash with the women. Before she became his wife, Virginia worried almost as much about female competition as she did the Japanese.

He waved off all the others and came back to her. But if he were around on August 6, he wouldn't be smiling. He would be miffed at all those who exposed him as a hero.

(November 30, 1984/July 23, 1986)

The battleship was a symbol
of stability . . .

Leonard Clanton was back from the wars as a Seabee and was being discharged when the Battleship *Wisconsin* returned from the Pacific and docked in San Francisco. On Navy Day, October 27, 1945, the ship's newspaper, *The Badger*, put out a special edition. Clanton visited a friend on the ship and picked up a copy of the paper.

It is a sort of yearbook of the *Wisconsin's* war record. There are pictures of the ship leaving the Philadelphia Naval Yard on its commissioning, a visit by Fleet Adm. Chester W. Nimitz inspecting the "*Wiskey*," as her crew called her. There are pictures of an aerial attack and the shooting down of three suicide planes off Okinawa, a map showing all the stops and battles of the *Wisconsin*, and scenes of the ship in rough seas. There are pictures of the crew at church and at dress inspections. There are pictures of sailors and U.S. Marines preparing to occupy the Japanese naval base at Yokosuka prior to the formal surrender and of Americans and Canadians repatriated from Japanese prison camps.

And there is a wealth of statistical information. Each day the crew of 3,000 officers and men consumed 4,110 pounds of vegetables, 1,640 pounds of fruit, 1,500 pounds of flour, 2,465 pounds of meat, 164 pounds of butter, 540 dozen eggs, 820 bars of candy, 875 quarts of ice cream, and 205 pounds of coffee and used 275 bars of soap.

The ship traveled 120,000 miles during the war. Its speed was more than 31 knots. Length, 880 feet, 3 inches. Width, 108 feet, 3 inches. Keel to foremast, 20 decks. Overall height, 186 feet, $2\,^1/_2$ inches. Horsepower in engines, 212,000. Fuel consumed April 16, 1944, to September 1, 1945, 22,641,518 gallons. Rounds of ammunition fired, more than 314,000. Paint needed to cover the ship, 312,000 pounds.

The *Wisconsin* joined the Third Fleet at Ulithi on December 9, 1944, was in the Leyte operations and Luzon attacks in December 1944 and January 1945, Formosa attacks, China Coast attacks, the Nansei Shota attack, the Iwo Jima assault, Tokyo carrier attacks, the raid against Honshu, and the Okinawa conquest, and was bombarding the Japanese homeland at the time of the surrender.

Admirals included Rear Adm. E. W. Hanson, Vice Adm. L. E. Denfield, and Rear Adm. H. F. Kingman. Commanding officers were Commodore E. E. Stone and Capt. J. W. Roper.

The paper printed a Navy Day proclamation by President Harry Truman honoring four million Americans who served in the Navy, Marine Corps, and Coast Guard.

"To them we owe our victory in the greatest naval war in history—a victory which destroyed two enemy fleets and placed our forces on the beachheads of final triumph."

He invited civilians to visit ships and planes that would be made available in cities around the country.

The masthead of the paper has a sketch of a battleship with a sailor holding aloft the American flag while pushing the Rising Sun of Japan into the ground. On the side is a helmet with a hole in it and a rifle stuck in the ground holding a banner that reads "Unconditional Surrender."

The *Wisconsin* was a busy ship during the relatively short time of its war service and quickly made its mark in the war.

Those aboard small craft always looked up to the battlewagons. The smaller vessels plowed through some waves and bounced over others. The battleship was a symbol of stability, where sailors wore undress blues and didn't often get wet. The dungaree Navy veterans will be looking forward to getting a look a the old *Wiskey*

(*July 9, 1985*)

[Editor's note: In 2001 the Battleship *Wisconsin* became a U.S. Naval Museum at Hampton Roads, Virginia. The ship remained part of the mothballed fleet.]

'Jettison your bombs and return to base. The war is over.'

"I cut off the power and I was right in the middle of this cane field..."

"So the controller says, 'Mister, if you plan to land here, I suggest you put your wheels down...'"

"I set down and turned right at the first intersection and my engine died. The radio said, 'Are you requesting a tractor?'"

The cocktail party of the ninth reunion of the 86th Torpedo Bomber Squadron of the Carrier *Wasp* was warming up at the Sheraton Marina Hotel. The boyish, trim pilots and crew members of 1945 are now greying and thicker.

"God, you look terrible," one greeted another.

The closeness of men who have survived was re-established. Wives of the group are just as close. They, too, endured together. These were the men of the second *Wasp*, dubbed "*The Stinger*." The first sank in the Battle of Guadalcanal.

Commissioned in 1943, *Wasp* launched air strikes against Marcus Island and Wake and then was off to bomb Tinian, Rota, and Guam and fight in the Battle of the Philippine Sea. In action off Kure Island, an armor-piercing bomb crashed through the flight deck, through two more decks, and exploded in the hangar deck, where the crew was lined up for chow. More than a hundred died. Many were wounded. The other half of the squadron was off on a strike. They were unaware many of their friends were dead.

"I was safe," Billie Easley, host for the reunion, said. "I was in my sack asleep."

"We were standing in the wardroom," Robert Wright recalled, "when a plane exploded below. Shrapnel made a colander of the deck. Lt. Harshbarger's leg was blown off below the thigh. I carried him out to the deck and tried to get help. We weren't trained to handle situations like that. Finally I got a medic. It was too late."

Albert T. Harshbarger, like many others in the group, was

trained at NAS Corpus Christi. He married a local girl and listed the city as his home.

"They put a big piece of steel over the hole in the flight deck, and we didn't know the ship had been hit until we landed and were lowered to the hangar deck," Bob Blu remembers.

The torpedo bombers used no torpedoes late in the war. They dropped bombs on the Japanese fleet at Kure Island. Ground fire was heavy and there were more losses.

"We were heading in for another strike on Japan," Easley remembers. "I had switched on my main tank and jettisoned my wing tanks when the radio said, 'Jettison your bombs and return to base. The war is over.'"

"Yeah," Wright said, "our fighter cover above us started cutting up, diving and rolling and dropping their bombs right through our formation. The commanding officer chewed them out."

But the war wasn't quite over for the *Wasp*. The war's last kamikaze exploded under its bow, lifting it high in the air and dropping it, shaking a crew that had visions of home. And the planes of the 86th had more bombing missions to fly, this time to prisoner-of-war camps, where many victims were near death from starvation.

"They came out of their barracks and waved to us," Gail B. (Spider) Young said. "We could see their gaunt, skinny bodies. They raised their arms to us. We dropped food, medicine, clothing, and some booze. On our next run they spelled out letters on the roof with torn sheets. It said, 'Bataan, Corregidor Prisoners Thank Wasp.'

"That sight somehow made those whole four years worthwhile."

(July 31, 1981)

To D-Day and Beyond

Photograph courtesy of the Corpus Christi Museum of Science and History: John Fred'k "Doc" McGregor Collection

Seventeen years before she would be sunk in one of the most unusual naval battles of World War II, the USS *Borie* enters the brand new Port of Corpus Christi.

Flags waved, bands played, and the decks of the USS *Borie* gleamed as she steamed up the ship channel to open the Port of Corpus Christi September 13, 1926. It was a moment of glory. In November 1943 the *Borie* would sink in another burst of glory in one of the strangest engagements in the history of naval warfare.

When the port opened, thousands of spectators crowded the shore around the Bascule Bridge. Local dignitaries and many more citizens stood on the dock and proclaimed the port officially opened as the ship passed under the bridge.

The celebration lasted for days before the *Borie* and destroyers *John D. Edwards* and *Hatfield* left port. The *Borie*, under command of Lt. Cmdr. George E. Brant, had completed a world tour, touching most of the ports of Europe, the Mediterranean, and the Middle and Far East. She helped American nationals in the China civil war and rendered earthquake assistance to victims in Yokohama.

Built in 1920, the four-stack destroyer was part of the nation's first-line sea defense. By World War II she was old and ready for retirement, but the Navy needed everything afloat. She was assigned convoy duty in the Atlantic.

Before one convoy reached Gibraltar, it was attacked by German *U-Boat 405*. The *Borie* gave chase, dropping patterns of depth charges. One of the depth charges damaged the submarine, causing it to surface directly in front of the destroyer. Lt. Charles H. Hutchins, her captain, ordered full speed to ram the U-Boat before its guns were manned. The *Borie's* bow climbed the *U-405's* foredeck and the two vessels locked together as John Paul Jones' *Bonhomme Richard* had locked with England's HMS *Serapis* in 1779. The gun crews were unable to depress their 4-inch guns enough to fire at the sub. The Germans swarmed on deck, and the battle continued with machine guns, rifles, shotguns, and pistols.

One of the American seamen threw his sheath knife, burying it in the stomach of a German sailor. The *Borie's* men dropped empty shell casings and anything else they could find on the Germans. The battle raged for ten minutes. The bow of the old destroyer began to buckle. The submarine commander threw his engines into reverse. The ship's hull collapsed, allowing the sub to pull free. It was too battered to submerge.

The *Borie* began to take on water as the vessels circled, each trying to ram the other. Hutchins called the engine room for flank speed. Engineers, some with water to their chest, worked in the dark to give their old ship one more burst of power. It brought the ship close enough for the crew to fire its K-gun depth charges. The explosives, set for shallow detonation, hurled through the air and straddled the sub, finishing it off. Its crew abandoned ship before it sank. Seas rose and the *Borie*, too, capsized and sank, carrying twenty-seven men with her. The survivors and the Germans were picked up by other destroyers.

If the saga sounds familiar, it is the story line used in the 1957 motion picture *The Enemy Below*, with Robert Mitchum and Curt Jurgens matching wits as rival captains.

I am indebted to Dick O'Keefe of the Corpus Christi State University Library, who wondered whatever happened to the *Borie* and asked researcher Helen Royal to find out.

Ms. Royal discovered that the movie didn't add a bit of excitement to the true life adventure of the USS *Borie* and her crew.

(*January 29, 1982*)

The submarine machine gunned and killed most of the men.'

When Peter Clark's ship was torpedoed in the North Atlantic during World War II, his lowly status saved his life.

"I was a bos'n's pig," he said. "I washed dishes, made beds, and did all the dirty jobs. They put me at the front of the lifeboat—the wet spot. A submarine surfaced, and its captain sounded so English we thought we were being rescued by an English submarine.

"But he was German. He took our captain aboard. Men were standing in the boats, pushing me down in the bow. The submarine machine gunned and killed most of the men. Four were badly shot up. Two died before we were picked up two days later. Only eight of us out of forty-three survived.

"I later heard the German captured captains of a number of ships he sank. As the sub returned to its base on the English Channel, it was sunk by British aircraft. Its crew and all the captains drowned."

I learned he ran away from his Canadian home at fourteen and went to sea. It was 1942—a bad year for ships in the North Atlantic. In England the war caught up with him again as he manned guns against dive bombers on the docks of Liverpool and London, the hottest action he saw. He sailed the North Atlantic and participated in troop landings in Italy. After the war he helped evacuate Nanking. He sailed the China coast and Japan and became a captain in 1958.

"I went through every stage of a seaman. There aren't many captains around today who can splice a cable."

In 1955 he was a whaler off the Australian coast. "That's one period of my life I am not proud of at this time, for I am now a conservationist. But the experience was to be valuable when I entered the seismic exploration business in 1960 because I knew the waters as well as anyone."

He was working that area when young Michael Rockefeller disappeared during a river trip in New Guinea.

"I participated in the search. They said he was eaten by crocodiles. I am convinced he was captured by cannibals. I found some canoes floating in a river. In them were the remains of villagers who had been killed by cannibals. I learned they raided an area only once in a great many years. In effect, people in remote villages were considered 'crops' by the raiders, not to be overharvested."

In the Fiji Islands he met a Japanese colonel who was recovering bodies of Japanese soldiers who had been buried during World War II.

"He said the spirits of the dead directed him to the graves. I know he had to have some sort of direction, for the jungle had reclaimed the area cleared out by the war. He would go right to the spot and have his crews dig. He said American soldier spirits had sent him to their graves. He sent their dog tags and bones home.

"At Biak thousands of miles away, I ran into him again. Here Americans were unable to reach Japanese troops in a deep system of caves. So they sealed the entrances and left them. When the caves were opened, it was obvious the trapped men had turned to cannibalism. Some bones were neatly stacked. Then the others saw they would die and committed hara-kiri."

I was glad to get a few sea stories out of the old sea dog.

(March 17, 1981)

'We landed in a swamp and a lot of our guys drowned.'

In the movie *The Longest Day*, the story of the Normandy invasion, American paratroopers dropped over Sainte Mére Eglise, France, at midnight before the invasion fleet hit the beaches on June 6, 1944.

"If things had been as easy as they were in the movie, we would have been all right," Victor Castillo recalls. "The 505th landed over town. Their chutes hung up on churches, buildings, and telephone poles. The Germans shot them and let them hang. I was with the 505th (part of the 82nd Airborne Division). We landed in a swamp and a lot of our guys drowned. Gliders took more casualties than we did. The Germans had raised railroad ties and tracks at an angle so the gliders would crash into them.

"It was pure havoc. We had those little cricket clickers for recognition. You'd click once and someone would answer with two clicks. The Germans found out about this and made a clicking sound with their knives on their rifle butts. Our guys would click. The Germans would click-click back, then shoot. Pretty soon, our guys were shooting each other.

"Gen. Matthew Ridgeway was in command, and Gen. Jim 'Slim' Gavin was our commander. He was a young, courageous man—one the men would die for. The weather threw us off, but we finally regrouped. Any troopers we came across were assigned to the 82nd. Then we were in fine form."

Castillo enlisted at eighteen. He was in North Africa and made his first combat jump into Sicily. It was there he earned the Silver Star. A German Panzer division was waiting for them and opened up on the floating paratroopers.

Castillo was hit in the leg. Some of the troop-filled planes were shot down by Navy gunners who mistook the transports for German planes. He carried a wounded comrade to a wine cellar. An Italian woman sprinkled sulfa powder on their wounds.

"We were in that wine cellar three days. We drank enough wine to ward off infection. But my leg turned green and stank to high heaven. I thought I was going to lose it, but they had penicillin and the doctors saved it."

He missed the drop over Salerno but was well enough for Anzio Beach, which took a terrible toll of American troops. After Anzio came D-Day and a number of other assaults. He earned eight battle stars and wings for three combat jumps. Next was the assignment to capture the bridge near Nijegen in Holland.

"We had a rough time in Holland. The weather was against us. We had little ammo left, no supplies. We were cold and wet and our boots were worn out. We cut up our blankets and wrapped them around our legs to keep from freezing."

Casualties among English, Canadian, Polish, and American troops were heavy.

"It wasn't easy on the Germans, either," he said.

The Germans were trying to get a column of heavy armor across the bridge, but they were beaten back before they could reach it and the Allies didn't have to blow it up. In December his unit was at Bastogne in the Battle of the Bulge and helped drive the Germans back when the weather cleared.

After the war Castillo joined the Navy. He served in Korea and was wounded early in the Vietnam War. He retired after twenty-seven years.

Friday the Southwest Airborne will begin a three-day reunion at La Quinta Royale. Medal of Honor winner Roy P. Benavidez will be Saturday's guest speaker.

"A lot of my old friends from the 82nd will be here," Castillo said.

A great many others will not. They lie in Africa, Sicily, Italy, France, Belgium, Holland, and Germany.

(June 6, 1984)

'Nobody had inspected our medical supplies between the two world wars.'

Dr. H. Gordon Heaney now lives in an old Army camp—Camp Scurry. Well, his home is where the World War I camp once was located.

"I was fascinated by the camp," he said. "I was eleven years old, and my mother would take me to the mess hall to give lessons to the soldiers. She was born in England but grew up in Paris where my grandfather had a farm implement businesses. I learned French as a child. We would have conversations in French so they would know basic language when they got overseas. The camp extended from the bay past Santa Fe and over to Southern Street on both sides of the Louisiana Ditch. The latrines were arranged on the edge of the ditch."

He had his own chance at soldiering at Roswell Military Institute.

"I figured that if I was going to be there, I might as well join the real Army. I joined the 56th Cavalry Brigade at El Paso when I was seventeen. I loved horses and learned to shoot a pistol from horseback, but it wasn't at all what I expected. I only stayed in long enough for my father to buy me out."

His father didn't buy him out of medical school. He was in the Chicago University School of Medicine when the Depression hit.

"I called home and my father answered. He told me never to call home again collect. Furthermore, I no longer lived in their house, though I was welcome to visit a few days at a time. Also, times were bad, and I could expect no further financial assistance.

"I went out and got a job washing dishes. A man came up and said if I didn't have a card, I'd have an accident on the way home. I told him I needed the job. The boss gave him a dollar, and I got a card saying I was a member of the Chicago Dishwashers and Scullery Union."

Later the university employed him as a research fellow, and he finished his training in medicine.

As a World War II Army doctor in North Africa, he was to

remember the old Camp Scurry when tents of the same vintage were set up there. In his first action he was rushed through artillery fire to the 10th Field Hospital. He opened his medical supply trucks and found them filled with French abortion instruments from the World War I era.

"There wasn't an instrument I could use. All we could do was put pressure on the wounds and call for a convoy of ambulances. Nobody had inspected our medical supplies between the two world wars."

On one occasion he watched artillery batter his grandfather's home. It was housing a German 88-millimeter battery. He found his grandfather's implement company and inquired about relatives. The manager offered to hide him for the duration of the war. He gave the man money to forward a message to his grandfather. It was never delivered. His grandfather had escaped Paris and was safe in London.

Dr. Heaney went through North Africa, Sicily, and Southern France. Later during his medical career he visited much of the area on a world tour.

He has recovered from a fractured back. A year ago he broke a vertebra lifting something heavy.

"I was on a half-track once that ran over a German mine," he said. "Three of my men up front suffered broken backs. I can now sympathize with the pain they endured."

(December 4, 1979)

Cartoons in the Army newspaper raised Patton's ire.

Everybody liked cartoonist Bill Mauldin in World War II —except Gen. George S. Patton. Virgil Pfeifer, who is drumming up business for the 45th Division's reunion in August, said Mauldin was in the 45th Division and was drafted to work on the division newspaper.

"Mauldin had been in combat a while with the 180th Infantry and later was at the front getting material for the newspaper," Pfeifer said. "He had gone on active duty on September 16, 1940, when the National Guard division was activated. The famous newspaper columnist Ernie Pyle took a liking to him and his cartoon characters, Willie and Joe. So he was drafted from drawing pictures for the regiment, then for the division, and finally in Italy for *Stars and Stripes*."

It was the cartoons in the Army newspaper that raised Patton's ire. He didn't think enlisted men should be allowed to make fun of officers. One cartoon showed two officers looking at the sun setting over the mountains. "Wonderful view," one said. "Is there one for enlisted men?"

"Of course, General Eisenhower liked Mauldin, so it didn't matter what Patton thought," Pfeifer said. "Mauldin had his own jeep and had the run of the place. At the invasion of France, the Air Corps flew him from Italy, jeep and all. He attended a couple of our reunions but hasn't been back for a few years."

In 1939 at age fifteen, Pfeifer joined the Oklahoma National Guard, which was activated along with the Texas 36th Division. The 45th, he said, was in the line 519 days. He was an infantryman and later a forward artillery observer. The most famous battle of the 45th was Anzio, during which the division bore the brunt of the German attack.

"Axis Sally said, 'You boys had better learn to swim because we're coming.' She was right, too. They were out to wipe us out with massive artillery. Our own artillery and that of the Navy saved us. After the battle only remnants of the outfit were left before the Germans were stopped," he said.

After the Italian campaign the 45th landed in Southern France. The division helped liberate the Dachau prison camp.

"We saw all the corpses. It made a believer out of me. Boxcars contained bodies of those who must have starved to death. They had turned the prisoners loose on the SS guards, and they mutilated them. There was a red brick cottage and a kindergarten next to the crematorium, which was some distance from the prison. This was the training center for the other death camps. Auschwitz had a much greater volume of executions."

At Munich, he said, the BMW automobile plant was partially intact. He went into the showroom and found photographs in a desk. "There were pictures of Hitler and Rudolph Hess looking at new cars. The Fuehrer was looking at cowhide seat covers. They were wearing swastikas."

This reminded him that the 45th Division, which wore the arrowhead shoulder patch, had worn swastikas, only they were the Indian good luck sign, the reverse of the Nazi symbol.

He has been contacting members of his old outfit. From a roster at Munich, he has located thirty living and eighteen deceased who had survived the war. He has located widows or children of the eighteen. There were 100 names on the roster. He is still looking for survivors or family members of those in the 45th Division. There are always a lot of widows and children wanting to hear about their husbands or fathers.

(June 16, 1987)

'Patton became a symbol to rally behind.'

Maj. Richard (Dick) Johnson was a tank officer in World War II and an instructor in tanks at Fort Knox until his retirement in 1960. He graduated from the Army's first tank school and joined Gen. George Patton's command.

"The movie *Patton* gave a pretty good portrayal of the way he was. He paced when he spoke. Only he spoke in a high-pitched voice. When he was angry, it was even more high pitched," Johnson said.

"He was a tall, well-built man. Every thing he wore was highly polished—his boots, belt, helmet, everything. He loved horses and polo. And he loved the cavalry. He was independently wealthy and didn't need the job. He was a showman. He earned three stars, but he wanted four. He was harder on officers than on enlisted men. He was tough, but inside he was a deeply religious man.

"The first time I met him I was holding a spring down with a pole as my men replaced a tank tread. Patton came up behind me. I couldn't let go and I couldn't salute.

"'More officers need to get their hands greasy,' he said."

When Patton took over the Second Army, he issued an order for officers to appear, seated, at 4 p.m.

"Those of us who knew him were seated. Those who didn't were standing up visiting before the general arrived. He had the names taken of all those standing. Then he said, 'Gentlemen. I do not speak with envy, but I do speak with authority. All of you have too much hair.' He was a little touchy about his own. There were a lot of haircuts on base.

"On maneuvers planes dropped sacks of flour to simulate bombs. Two of my tanks were knocked out. Patton asked what I was doing. I told him I was circling an enemy hill with two tanks."

"'Wipe the flour off those tanks. You can't learn anything with just two tanks.'

"Then a sergeant was sent into the cold river waters to determine the depth before the tanks crossed. Patton came up and marched into the water, shiny boots and all. He yelled, 'Lieutenant, get your (bleep) out of that tank and into this water!' The enlisted men appreciated that."

The general was always the rebel.

"General Bradley ordered that tanks would not use streets on the post. He went to Washington, and Patton drove the whole division up and down the streets so everyone would wake up as early as the troops."

And tanks were not supposed to use public highways. But Patton made the people of Panama City, Florida, happy about using theirs. He held a tank rodeo at the fair grounds. Traps, poles, and ramps were erected; and tanks raced, jumped, crashed, and demolished the set to the applause of townspeople, who had no complaints about tanks.

Johnson served in Europe with the First Army and Patton led the Third.

"He was rash and wanted to hit hard and surprise. Others learned from Rommel to use tanks first as artillery, then as tanks for greater effect. He may not have been the greatest general. But he became a symbol to rally behind. In that he was the greatest!"

(November 17, 1978)

They fought with German destroyers, corvettes, E Boats, R Boats, and F Lighters . . .

The Bible mentions turning swords into plowshares, but advertising executive Lon C. Hill III did the same thing with a typewriter. It came about when the famous war correspondent-columnist Ernie Pyle was a passenger on Hill's Patrol Torpedo Boat during the bloody Anzio Beachhead battle in early 1944.

"There were no 'copters in those days, so the PT Boats were water taxis when they weren't attacking German shipping," Hill recalls. "We took Ernie up from Naples to Anzio with some other passengers and brought him back with a load of badly wounded soldiers to the 24th General Hospital.

"He was already a legendary figure. He was a thin, wiry little guy who reminded you of Norman Rockwell. The sailors loved him. There were a couple of medics to attend the wounded on deck. The blankets were bloody. Many of the wounded hadn't even been bandaged.

"Ernie talked to them and comforted them. He walked alone in the open. He was without fear. That was to be his death from a sniper on an island in the Pacific. He did everything himself. There was no entourage with him.

"When we got back, he said I could have his old Underwood typewriter. He was getting a new one. He had used the old one for years in his travels across the country and later in Africa, Sicily, and Italy. A tripod folded into the bottom so he could sit on his helmet and type.

"I brought the battered old portable home with me. I was working for J. M. Mathis Advertising Co. on Madison Avenue. We and everyone else were trying hard for the Underwood account. I donated Ernie Pyle's old machine for their company archives. I don't know whether that influenced them or not. But it certainly got their attention."

That run also involved another important passenger aboard the PT 233, Hill recalls—Lt. Gen. Mark Clark.

"We fired our entire supply of Very recognition flares at an advancing U.S. minesweeper en route to Anzio. Three-inch shells splashed about and hit us. The AM-120, fresh over from the States, was convinced we were a German E-Boat out to sink them even though we were coming from Allied territory.

"When the sweeper finally ceased fire, General Clark ordered us alongside the smoking three-inchers and called the ship's captain to the rail. 'Commander,' he raged, 'you have just inflicted the first casualties of the day. Congratulations. Only they are American boys. Be at my command post at 0800 hours.' The AM-120 had a new commanding officer within hours."

Hill has prepared a number of anecdotes about the activities of MTB Ron 15 in the Mediterranean for a former squadron commander who is preparing a book on PTs. One tale which I heard when officers of Patrol Torpedo Boat Squadron 15 met here a few years ago involved Lt. Hal Nugent on PT 210, which picked up a target on radar coming from the direction of the Allied landing convoy.

The 210 challenged the target with the day's secret blinker light and received the correct response. The PT pulled alongside what it took to be a landing craft lost from the invasion fleet. Nugent walked to the bow wearing his binoculars and carrying his megaphone to ask the name and number of the vessel. The reply was an old-fashioned broadside from a German F-Lighter, an armed barge-like craft. Its 88- and 20-millimeter cannons opened up at point-blank range. The blast blew away Nugent's megaphone, snapped the binoculars strap, jammed the wheel, and knocked out the engine controls, leaving the boat dead in the water. Nugent ordered his crew to commence firing, and the return fire disabled the German vessel. If I remember, the other officers gave him the name "Bullhorn" Nugent.

The war fought by PT Ron 15 was unique in World War II. It compared to the old sea battles of ship against ship, except for the regular bombing attacks. They fought battles with German destroyers, corvettes, E Boats, R Boats, and F Lighters, all of them heavily armed. From April 1943 until September 1944, their log was one of almost daily patrols and clashes, usually under hostile shore batteries in the Mediterranean.

Most of the talk at the reunion was about the funny things officers of that group remembered. Some of the sea stories were great. Torpedoes that didn't fire or fired but ran erratically were a recurrent problem. One boat took a torpedo in the transom, through the lazarette and the aft crews quarters, stopping inches short of 3,000 gallons of high-octane gasoline. An alert torpedoman grabbed a towel and jammed it in the impeller, bringing it to a stop seconds before it would have armed and blown the boat to smithereens.

I asked Capt. S.M. Barnes about the erratic torpedo.

"Actually, it wasn't erratic. We had a new officer, so we put him back in tail-end Charlie position. When things opened up, he got excited and dropped a fish a little prematurely."

The damaged boat limped back to base as other boats fought off pursuers.

Another story involved rockets someone had ordered installed as a test. Rockets smashed the target, but a dozen or so would misfire, remaining on the launch fully armed and ready to explode at a touch. Each was lowered carefully overboard with fishing line. Protests that the rockets weren't safe got no audience until Capt. Barnes went on patrol. He personally kicked the racks overboard, ending the experiment.

Waldo Frank, a civilian sent to install radar, couldn't get clearance to go home. He handed his draft notice to the skipper, who said, "You'll go home when I go home."

At that time the Navy had no radarmen. Frank endured daily bombings, repairing radar units while his draft board wondered where he was.

Leland "Boomer" Page got his nickname when a British corvette couldn't understand his East Texas dialect. In frustration, he threw his bullhorn overboard, shouted (with profanity) across the open sea and was heard perfectly.

In August 1943 three of Hill's PT Boats joined with the destroyer *Trippe* to capture the entire group of Lipari Islands, taking seventy-five prisoners of war.

However, Hill admits, when he had his opportunity to capture a Nazi-held Mediterranean island, he "blew it." As the Allies were invading the southern coast of France in 1944, "we could have used schooling in the fine art of taking prisoners and accepting surrenders," he wrote.

Lt. Ed DuBose, skipper of the 213 Boat, had been hailed as "The Commandant" by the residents of the island of Stromboli.

"But Ed was nowhere to be found when Vice Admiral Henry K. Hewitt from ... the cruiser USS *Augusta* told me I was 'volunteering' for a truce mission to accept the surrender of the German-held island of Poquerolle, which had been bypassed by the advancing Allies.

"Naval Intelligence had the Germans in possession of a gigantic Russian mortar which would affect our use of the big French naval base in Toulon. We had to capture it. The admiral felt Jerry would give up if he knew he was bypassed and U.S. forces were already in Toulon.

"Our Truce Party, under the command of Col. W. C. Baxter, included an Army intelligence officer, a Navy interpreter, a communications specialist, and war correspondent George Tucker, representing the combined American press."

On August 8, 1944, Tucker wrote, "It was a sunshiny afternoon on the Riviera as the little PT Boat with white flags flying pointed her nose toward the goal. Two large white flags were prominently displayed on deck and couldn't be mistaken for anything but truce flags. Gunners were not at their station for obvious reasons . . .

"The harbor is near the west end of the island, and anything approaching it must come under the muzzles of the peninsula's shore batteries . . . the Germans could certainly see us . . . If we were going to draw fire, this seemed to be the moment. But no fire came. The boat seemed to relax. But as we drew up to the harbor entrance and turned to enter, the Germans opened fire. Muzzles flared on the hillside. Baxter, the party CO, flung himself face down on the deck, as did the rest of the party.

"'Let go! Let me go! Someone's squeezing me around the middle,' the interpreter yelled . . . He hit the deck so hard he activated the CO^2 cartridges in the automatic lifebelt around his waist, inflating it instantly.

"There was considerable cursing and rolling about by the party while Hill, who commanded the torpedo boat, swung her in a sharp arc as he ordered smoke and headed back through the narrow channel we had blazed on the way in.

"The Germans' first salvo was the closest thing they threw at us. One or two degrees lower and it would have been a direct hit. As it was, high explosives whistled and sang as they whammed past our heads. Hill zig-zagged twice, smoke billowing from our stern . . .

"Long before we got back to the flagship, battleships and cruisers began to converge from different points of the horizon and slammed high explosive shells into the peninsula where the Germans violated the white flag of truce."

The Germans had allowed the boat to come in so far their 88-millimeter cannons could not depress far enough to hit the speeding boat.

Hill said he visited Poquerolle Island in 1984 and found it is a popular sunbathing and nudist colony.

"For guys accustomed to patrolling in the dark of moon," he said, "we felt awfully 'exposed' there that sunny afternoon."

(January 26, 1983/June 23, 1987)

'We broke out of the beachhead on D-Day plus two...'

Old times came flooding back to Frank Flores when he picked up his newspaper last Friday. There on the front page was a picture of President Carter and French President Giscard d'Estaing standing on the bluff of Omaha Beach on the Normandy Coast. Another picture showed American troops climbing the bluff on D-Day, June 6, 1944.

"The fourth GI on the right is me," Flores said. "In the lead is Sgt. Simpson. I saw him in San Antonio twenty years ago. Next is Sgt. Grizzle. He was killed. I can't recognize the next guy."

It was I Company, 23rd Infantry Regiment, Second Infantry Division. Of the 140 men in the company, all but 40 were to be casualties of the war.

"We were on the transport all the night before. There was a lot of activity in the air and on the beach. An enemy fighter plane came over, and all the ships opened up. The tracers lit up the sky so much you could see the plane real clear.

"The landing craft were under fire on the way in to the beach. They didn't go in far enough. When they opened the door, it went under water. It should have been on the bottom. We jumped into the water. It was cold—and ten feet deep. I had a hundred pounds of ammo on my back. I grabbed a rope and walked out on the bottom. Some of the guys drowned there. Some of them got hit. We lost ten on the beach. We couldn't fire back at the snipers who were shooting at us while we were in the water because our rifles were covered in plastic bags."

The men were walking single file when the picture was taken, under the protection of the bluff.

"When we topped the hill and got to the woods, 88s, 75s and everything else opened up. We were pinned down for half a day and lost a bunch of guys. We were glad when the tanks caught up with us so we could get behind them. We broke out of the beachhead on D-Day plus two and captured a village two miles inland. A big house was Nazi headquarters. They left papers, rifles—everything. The guys picked up a bunch of souvenirs. I had a duffel bag full, but I gave it all away to relatives."

Three weeks later a sniper shot him in the back, leg, and wrist. His war was over. He was eighteen years old.

I asked what medals he earned. There was the Purple Heart, Presidential Unit Citation, "and the Good Conduct Medal."

"I didn't get a chance to get to Paris and get in trouble," he laughed. "The memories of it all come up every so often. There was the war, girls, the good things, and the bad things. They get all mixed up. But the bad things aren't nearly so bad as they were at that time."

The photograph in the newspaper brought back some of the bad he hadn't thought of in thirty-two years.

"It was like the past caught up with me all of a sudden," he said.

(January 13, 1978)

'... there were ships as far as you could see...'

After forty years of trying, A.G. Ryan has finally received a discharge for his service in World War II. He served aboard a small tanker carrying high-octane fuel to refuel patrol craft during the invasion of Normandy.

"The problem is they could never figure out what branch of the service I was in," Ryan said.

Before the battle he was a civilian in the employ of the Army Transport Service.

"Since we were going to be under fire, they decided to swear us in under the Articles of War. The uniform I wore was almost identical to that of a Navy officer, except the hat bore the insignia of the Army Transport Service. Yet I wasn't exactly in the Army. The uniform had three stripes on the shoulder, and everyone who saw me swore I was in the Navy," he said.

"The question came up. Was I in the service or not? I guess it took an act of Congress to get something started. Wright Patman wrote a letter to the Army for me, and they sent me forms and information. I filled them out and mailed them, and that would be all I'd hear. Through the years I'd write and ask about the status of my discharge, and they would send me the same forms and papers to fill out, and nothing would happen. I have been in the American Legion even though I couldn't produce proof I was in the military."

He was working as an insurance adjuster in Seattle in 1943 when he was hired as an interviewer in the Army Transport Office. He assigned himself to the diesel engineering school. When he graduated, he was the equivalent of a second lieutenant, but he was still a civilian.

"I was sent to New Orleans to put a Y-26 tanker into service. I was promoted and would have been first lieutenant had I been in the service. The port commander asked me to take the ship to the European Theater of Operations. We nearly lost it in a storm off Florida. We entered the North Atlantic in a convoy but were separated from it when our main generator failed. We were a sitting duck for submarine attack, but we made it to England six months before the invasion.

"On the morning of D-Day, there were ships as far as you could see. The battleships throwing broadsides were the most impressive thing I've ever seen. We saw the first wave of landing craft as they approached Omaha and Utah beaches.

"Then a storm hit. We lost three anchors, but our ship wasn't damaged. Our sister ship went aground. The flares they dropped at night seemed like they were aiming for us. We were a floating bomb with all that hundred-octane gasoline," he said.

"We had Navy, Army, Marines, Merchant Marine, and civilians aboard the vessel. For the service before being sworn in, I received hazardous duty pay. One of the papers they sent me listed me as an ordinary seaman."

He received orders to return to the States and went home to Oklahoma to await further orders. He thought he would be transferred to the Pacific, but the war ended. No further orders came. He was never officially notified of his discharge, a fact that must have given the military bureaucrats something to puzzle over.

Then, last week, after he had despaired of ever receiving a written discharge, he received one from the government records facility in St. Louis. It says, "Honorable Discharge from the Armed Forces of the United States, a testimonial of honorable and honest service." Some military mind had solved the dilemma.

"They got the dates wrong," Ryan said, "but after forty years, I'm not going to complain."

(February 3, 1989)

'He told them to shoot us when we were 300 yards away.'

Knowing more than one language allowed Mrs. Reyna Hershberger to live and to hate prejudice. She spoke English, French, Italian, and German. It was German that kept her from being executed at the hands of Hitler's SS troops. She lived in Italy and was suspected of being Jewish. Her father was French and her mother Italian, but she had many Jewish friends.

"We were detained at the SS headquarters by the Gestapo. Many had already been sent to concentration camps. But they let me go when they found out I was a Gentile. They kept us in a square box for three days. I was with a cousin. I didn't let them know I could speak German.

"The commander told the soldiers to let the frauleins go. Then he told them to shoot us when we were 300 yards away. We walked fast. We kept a tree between us and the soldiers, then jumped into a ravine. They shot, but we ran to the mountains. They didn't follow us because Germans never came back from the mountains."

That made her a member of the Italian Partisans, a group that fought secretly against the Germans and Italian Fascists. She showed me silver medals she had won at school for marching and rifle marksmanship. One pictured the Italian Fascist Party symbol and a likeness of dictator Benito Mussolini.

"The Italian Fascists arrested people, gave them castor oil, and beat them with clubs," she said, "but they were nothing compared to the SS and the Gestapo. We helped a lot of Jewish people hide in the mountains. One family flew a flag on their roof to show they were all right. One day it was gone. We found all shot, women and children, too. We buried them. Every time one German was killed, they killed ten Italians. For a sergeant it was thirty. An officer was worth fifty Italians."

Once she helped plant explosives in a trash can in an SS camp.

"We waited in the hills with binoculars. When they changed the guard, they pushed the plunger. It blew twelve of them up. They killed 450 civilians in reprisal. You must do these things to be free."

She was wounded once in the leg by shrapnel and was buried alive eighteen hours after an air raid.

"Water was up to our necks. The Germans weren't going to dig us Italians out until they heard a German cry for help, too. There was an unexploded bomb in the hole with us."

Later the Partisans were between the American and German armies for forty days.

"We sabotaged communications, roads, and railroads. The Germans by the river killed everybody in their path when they came out. A Prussian with a machine gun was robbing people. A farmer killed him. We buried him and were uneasy. But they never missed him. I was nearby when they shot Mussolini, but I didn't see it. The Americans were mad that we had done that.

"My father was in charge of police for King Immanuel. He didn't sympathize with Mussolini. Every day after school he would tell us why our political teachers were wrong. My father was a Renault. He was a fourth generation huntsman. He ran 400 dogs for families all over Europe. We managed to save many of our Jewish friends. One of them, a dentist, fixed my teeth the last time I was in Italy.

"It taught me to hate prejudice. I am dark and have been mistaken for Mexican and was refused a house on the Southside. I understand prejudice, but I don't like it. All you have to do is remember what it did to the Germans and the Jews."

(May 9, 1978)

'We got to the Ardennes just as the Germans came in.'

Al Pennine is a little guy with a stiff back, bad feet, and luck that's been no better. He goes to the health club on doctor's orders to take light exercise and build up his strength. Sometimes he feints and jabs the air with his fists. And when he talks, you can almost hear the slap of leather, the bounce of punching bags, and the smell of sweat and liniment of the boxers' training gym.

"According to my count, I had forty-nine fights," he said, "and only lost nineteen. My top fight was against the AAU champ, Nicki Wargo. I weighed 126 pounds. I decked him in the second round. His brother threw in the towel, but I didn't get to a neutral corner. He came out in the third round. I wasn't aggressive enough and he won the decision. That was in 1943."

But he didn't get the bad back, the bad feet or even the dent in his head in the ring. In 1944 he took an even worse beating. He enlisted in the Army. After six weeks in basic training, he landed in Marseilles and was rushed north.

"We got to the Ardennes just as the Germans came in. On December 16 we were bottled up. That's when they really hit us, 88's and every kind of artillery they had. It was the Battle of the Bulge, but we didn't know it. We didn't know anything. You couldn't believe how cold it was. Artillery was coming in. They told us if we could count to twenty, it wouldn't hit us."

Once the count didn't reach twenty and everything blew up. Al had a hole in the front of his helmet and a dent in his skull. Guys who got out of their foxholes were cut in two. Buddies were lying around everywhere.

"Ya know, the medics looked at me, and because I wasn't bleeding, I didn't get a Purple Heart."

"We lost track of time. I guess it was battle fatigue. We didn't have helmets and our feet were frozen. Somehow we got to an aid station. They wanted to take my feet off. I wouldn't let 'em. Notice sometimes my foot gives way. Can't feel it. It was January 7 when we got out."

He came home to a few more amateur fights.

"They gave us $3 to $10 under the table and some Spaulding sporting goods," he said. "I couldn't take much more. I had bad feet and gristle knuckles."

He had worked as a tile setter and became a union official and then a union negotiator. "I knew George Meany and all the officials," he said.

Then the union sent him to South Texas to organize.

"Things didn't go too well and they cut me loose, my good buddies. They nailed me. My local in Pittsburgh only had one vote. San Francisco had three. So they put their guy in. I was one year short of retirement benefits. They knew these things, my good buddies, but I'm not bitter."

He showed me his union card. The attached picture with dark hair looks like Vince Lombardi.

"A guy came up to me at the airport once and called me Vince. I said, 'Jeez, I wish I wuz, pal.'"

He pulled a numbers slip from his wallet. "Look at this. The number came up 38. I had 39, one number away from two thousand bucks."

"Hey," he said as he riffled through the wallet. "You should have seen me when I was young. They said I looked like John Garfield and what's that Palooka's name on the TV? Columbo. I really did."

He's retired now. He was working at NAS when he picked up a heavy box and ruptured a vertebra in his back.

Someone told him he should try to get his veteran's disability increased from the 10 per cent he has been getting. It hadn't occurred to him he might get more.

"I must be punchy," he grinned.

It's about time Al Pennine won one.

(November 21, 1988)

The prisoners were marched behind German lines to the Rhine River . . .

Henry Eskew had to work extra hard to keep up with the nineteen-year-olds he was training for World War II. He was thirty-six when he was drafted in 1943. He died in January 1988 at the age of eighty. While he was still in good health late in 1987, he wrote a journal of his experiences as a prisoner of war of the Germans and sent a copy to his nephew, James Eskew of Corpus Christi, Texas.

Henry Eskew was a training sergeant in the 232nd Infantry until December 1944, when he was sent to France, where he was assigned as machine gunner in the point jeep leading the 42nd Division. The unit helped capture Strasbourg and helped hold a line along the Rhine River.

"The 232nd took up the defense nineteen miles long. We were spread thin. We were cold and hungry."

They managed to fight the Germans back near the town of Kilstett.

"I had a machine gun in my arm, a bandolier of ammunition on my shoulder, an M-1 rifle, a .45 pistol on my side, and a full pocket of hand grenades . . . German soldiers were hiding low against a wall across the street. Just as we got even with them, they jumped up and began throwing hand grenades, rifle fire, and everything they had at us. The boys were falling and screaming. A shell hit the building where I was standing, and a part of the wall collapsed on me. The last thing I remember was the sound of my helmet rolling down the street.

" . . . when I woke up, I didn't have a thing. The Germans thought I was dead and had taken my machine gun, rifle, all my ammunition—everything . . . I could see the Germans in the moonlight, turning the boys over to see if they were dead and stripping them of their guns."

Germans captured him and were threatening to shoot him when American artillery opened up and the Germans threw him into a cellar with other prisoners. They were marched behind German lines to the Rhine River, where they were taken on a terrifying ride across the cold river in a small rowboat with less than an inch of freeboard.

"We were the first to get the new type combat boots and the Germans wanted them . . . They took our boots and gave us old shoes that wouldn't fit and emptied our pockets—took our watches, rings, everything."

They were taken to Stalag 13-C, where 1,000 prisoners were held. "Our shelter was an old mule barn. There was no heat and it was freezing. There was no light. You just had to feel your way around in the dark. We had several tubs we used as latrines."

They slept on lice-infested, straw-filled tow sacks.

"I was lucky. I didn't have much hair on my body, and I slept on the top bunk and didn't have lice dropping on me from the mattress above."

This was the best equipped of the many camps they would stay in. They were fed a tin cup of soup once a day and a slice of bread. "Every day many prisoners died. I can't even guess the number. We formed six-man burial details every morning to take the dead out and bury them."

The marches from camp to camp were difficult. The Germans were retreating and had little desire or few resources to care for prisoners. Once their train was derailed by an American bombing raid.

"The boy next to me had been telling me not to worry, that the war would be over soon. He was hit in the chest and died . . . In the last days of the war, we were moved more frequently. More often than not, there was no shelter, so we slept in the snow."

He lost fifty pounds in five months.

"Unexpectedly, American infantry appeared at the top of a hill. A guard ran past me, and I tackled him because I wanted his bayonet. I wonder why I took that chance minutes away from liberation."

Eskew was hospitalized many months before he could return to his service station job in Bastrop.

(January 19, 1988)

Thirty years ago
they were trying
to kill each other . . .

I've known these two guys for years. One is a German mechanic. The other is a tavern operator. They are friends on insulting terms:

"Dumb Kraut."

"He's got a big mouth."

They weren't always so friendly. Thirty years ago they were trying to kill each other, only they didn't know it.

S-Sgt. Vernon Krause was convinced he didn't have long to live. If the Germans didn't get him, the sub-zero weather would.

A few miles away 1st Lt. Heinz Bushchang, German fighter pilot, was shivering and thinking the same thing. He was grounded with an air-warning unit after American ack-ack shot down his plane, causing a head injury. He had been wounded earlier on the Russian front.

"A big drive was on," Heinz said. "There were brand new huge Tiger tanks of new design, the latest equipment, and the best soldiers in Germany, including a lot of SS men. We didn't know what it would mean to the war."

"They were the ugliest monsters you ever saw, those Tiger tanks," Vernon said. "They were painted white and came out at night. And we only had rifles to shoot at them. All you could do was hide and hope they didn't run over you. And the German infantry kept charging and we kept shooting. The snow was black with their bodies. It was cold. God, it was cold."

"We didn't have much of anything left," Heinz said. "There was no tobacco. No food. Not even ammunition. And it was so cold, you can't imagine how cold it was."

"We were surrounded for thirteen days," Vernon said. "The ground was frozen, and we couldn't bury the dead. On the night of Jan. 4, (1945) the 41st Armored Division broke through and got us out. They took us back and we got showers. The line was a mile long, and the showers were three minutes each. Then we went off for amphibious river-crossing practice."

"The German drive was aimed at an American fuel depot," Heinz said. "The tanks had no fuel. Even if I had not been injured,

I could not have flown because the planes were on the ground, out of gas. The tanks didn't reach the depot. They stopped on the roads and a lot were blown up. More were destroyed by Germans than Americans."

The Battle of the Bulge was over.

The 79th moved out again. Vernon was in on the retaking of the Siegfried Line and was in Boat 13 crossing the Rhine. He was decorated as the first soldier in his division to shoot a German soldier on German soil.

"They just overran us and we were captured," Heinz said. "On the Russian front it was kill or be killed. On the Western Front you could be captured, which is not such a bad alternative."

As a prisoner he was in charge of a transportation company working for the U.S. Army. He was released at a camp at Frankfurt, his home. He completed his mechanics training at a Mercedes-Benz plant and moved his family to Rochester, New York, in 1957. He moved to Corpus Christi in 1965 "to get away from the snow."

Vernon returned to his old job at Central Power & Light and started working in a drive-in grocery. Later he purchased the business known as Vernon's Carside Drive-in, a popular beer and barbecue spot. Heinz met Vernon "the second day I was here, looking for a watering place."

"Took me a while to get used to him. Thought he was a spy," Vernon said. "Didn't have much to do with him until once we sat down and had a few beers together. Now we go hunting together."

They don't talk much about the war.

"I say he was in the Red Ball Express (An American Army noncombat outfit)," Heinz said.

"He couldn't shoot, anyway," Vernon said. "He couldn't hit anything. I taught him to shoot. Then he shot redbirds, sparrows, and sometimes a dove. You know, I taught him to hunt. He doesn't do bad now."

"Red Ball Express," said Heinz.

You can tell they're friends. Otherwise they'd have shot each other years ago.

(January 1, 1975)

'Tanks broke down the barbed wire fences and the Germans surrendered.'

Stories have a way of changing when you chase them to their source. The way I heard it, this fellow was a prisoner of war in Germany and this German delivered mail to the prisoners. One day, back in Corpus Christi, this fellow looks up and there is this old German mailman delivering his mail in a U.S. Postal Service suit.

It was a good story but not quite accurate. The fellow was R. S. Carter, then a downed B-24 bomber pilot. The mailman was no German. He was David J. Alaniz, now retired from the U.S. Postal Service.

Carter doesn't think back on the prison camp experience as a terrible one. "I got in the Air Corps to keep from walking, but they (the Germans) marched us all over Germany, changing camps. There wasn't much food, but we were well treated when you think about the guys who survived the Bataan Death March. Those are the guys you should be talking to."

He was in Sagan Prison for a while. "That was where they sent the 'bad guys.' I could never figure out why I was sent there," Carter said. "Once we had five tunnels going. We told the Germans about four of them so they wouldn't find the fifth one. They let us dig because it kept us busy."

He was moved several times in 1945 as the war began to go badly for the Third Reich. He ended up at Moosburg, Germany.

Alaniz, wounded three times in combat in North Africa, Sicily, and Italy, was captured at Cassino. He compares his experience with the Bataan Death March. "We were marched for three months in freezing weather. At night we stood huddled together to keep from freezing. We seldom slept. We went eleven days without any food. When anyone lagged behind, he was shot. The guards had vicious German shepherds.

"Stalag A-7 at Moosburg was nearly empty when we arrived. It was a transient camp, so it began to fill up with prisoners from other camps. We were the cadre, so we set up the process for running the camp," Alaniz said.

His job was to sort and deliver mail to American prisoners. "I had to devise a system by which mail could be delivered to men in all sections of the prison. I had no idea I would ever be a mail carrier, but it was a pretty good system," he said.

He delivered German identification papers to Lt. Carter, who still has them.

As the end of the war approached, Gen. (Alexander) Patch rode into the camp in a tank to ask the German camp commander, Colonel Mulheim, to surrender. He refused and asked that the area seven miles around be declared neutral ground.

"General Patch cussed and roared off. He was back at daybreak, the tanks broke down the barbed wire fences, and the Germans surrendered. Across the way the Germans had killed sixteen carloads of Jews to keep them from being liberated," Alaniz said. "I had been afraid to shower in the concrete shower houses in the camp. They had gas nozzles in the ceiling for exterminating prisoners."

He was hospitalized for malnutrition, then flown back to the States. He and Carter flew out on the general's plane.

It took several years for the Army to get the prisoners' pay records straightened out. Then the government mailed Carter the pay he had accumulated as a prisoner. It was delivered by Alaniz. They had a Stalag reunion and see one another occasionally.

Sometimes the real story is just as good as the one you started out with.

(August 21, 1975)

The Wild Blue Yonder

A B-24 crew immediately after a raid on a German target. The airman on the far right is the author's brother, O.D. Walraven Jr., who flew thirty missions as a gunner in the 8th Air Force.

Most men who have been in war remember the good times. Memory tends to repress bad things in time, and fortunately for his sanity, the veteran cannot reconstruct the tiny details of combat and its stark horrors.

However, John Comer, who entered the service at the beginning of World War II, has managed to do just that. He was able to do it because he kept a daily journal, reconstructing the conversations, anecdotes about his comrades, and the sheer terror of the moment as he flew his first twenty-five missions in the 381st Bomb Group of the 8th Air Force. The year was 1943—not a good time at all to be beginning the high-level daylight bombing attacks on German targets. B-17 Flying Fortresses had not been perfected, and the men were only half trained.

The Allies had no fighter planes capable of long flights, and the German Luftwaffe had planes and experienced pilots waiting for the lumbering formations of bombers, knocking down forty, fifty, sixty bombers at a time, watching for stragglers and green bomber crews.

Comer captures the feeling of the times with chilling effect, starting with mission one and carrying it through twenty-five. His book, *Combat Crew*, was published by Texian Press.

My brother was a tail gunner who survived. I listened to his tales when he returned from the war. In Comer's work he and other survivors will find a diary of their own experiences they would otherwise be unable to recall.

Combat troops on the ground were more or less numbed by the dirt, discomfort, and unrelenting danger. The airmen were safe in England, in relative comfort. They had ice water showers and little heat, but they were inside and safe. Then, for several hours, they would be placed under the most trying psychological conditions possible—flak bursting, sending white-hot steel through the shell of the planes, German fighter planes attacking with cannon and rockets, men dying at their posts because of faulty oxygen equipment, others suffering frostbite in 40-below temperatures as they were blasted by 300-mph winds through open hatches and bomb bays. All the while they watched as plane after plane, many of them carrying friends, caught fire and spiraled to the ground. Those still aloft prayed they would see parachutes come from the falling wreckage. They seldom did.

These are generalities. Comer is specific. He gives you word-for-word conversations on the intercom as missions were flown in such suicidal attacks as those on the stoutly defended ball-bearing plants at Sweinfurt and others on Bremen, Leverkusen, Emden, Ludwigshafen—names that caused crews to groan on the days they were announced.

Even later in the war, with long-range escorts and a depleted Luftwaffe, surviving twenty-five missions would be no mean feat, but in 1943 the odds were much higher against it.

"The first thing they told us when we got there," Comer said, "was that the casualty rate was higher than 100 percent. We soon saw that was true."

Men who had survived nearly twenty-five missions suffered mightily, for so many were killed just before they reached that number. Comer later flew sixty missions in Italy. He was flight engineer and ball gunner. He made it. His best friends, who were several missions behind him, did not.

There were goof-ups in command that cost thousands of lives, but the bombings undoubtedly shortened the war. Comer believes they would have been more effective had they been concentrated on each target until it was wiped out.

"I wasn't interested in writing a great book about the war," he said. "I just recorded the small part of it that about twenty men saw."

It was all there—experiences such as trying to dislodge bombs stuck in the rack while standing with no parachute on the narrow catwalk over the open bomb bay. There was the time the tail gunner stored an extra supply of ammunition in the tail and the plane took off only after the pilot lowered the wheels and bounced in an open field, barely clearing trees before being airborne. There was the tail gunner turning black from lack of oxygen, the ball gunner with glass in his eyes after shrapnel hit his goggles, another man with shrapnel through his leg. There was the loss of their plane, which went down with another crew inadvertently assigned to it by a clerk. There was the jinx ship nobody wanted to fly, which finally went down with a German fighter halfway through it.

"I was surprised when I read my notes on the missions," he said. "I remembered none of that stuff, but as I read it, it all came back. We had a hard time sleeping, so I kept a journal. I put down all the conversations we had during missions and our discussions about it later. After every mission we'd talk and go over everything that happened. The men were from several different aircraft, and I wrote it all down. Later I couldn't remember what I had experienced and what I was told. It was all very similar."

He showed his notes to his old commanding officer, Lt. Col. Stuart S. Watson, and Watson suggested he make a book of it.

"Four years ago we went back to Rangewell Airdrome to dedicate a memorial," Comer said. "The landowner donated the land for the black granite monument. Mind you, this field was out in the country, eighteen miles from Cambridge. About 100 of us were there. We didn't expect anyone else to show up. More than 500 people from the villages came. They said they didn't want us to think they had forgotten. They wanted to show their appreciation. The English are a wonderful people."

He sent his book to several publishers without success. Texian Press encouraged him to cut it. He eliminated most of the training period and opted not to tell of furloughs in London.

"Some of those people might be preachers now," he said, smiling.

As a result, he captured the immediacy of the situation.

"Couldn't rely on my memory," he said. "Things I thought I knew, I didn't after I looked at the journal. If there was a court trial of something that happened ten years ago and I was a juror, I don't think I would take the word of any of the witnesses."

The reality of his account has had an impact on other former airmen who have read it. They say their experiences were exactly the same.

"A P-47 fighter pilot called me to say he read it all the way through," Comer said. "He said, 'I always wondered what you guys were doing down there.'"

Comer named his first-born son after his two best friends, who were killed on the same day, January 11, 1944. And as the diaries stirred memories of all those lost, he knew he had to write the book so they would not be forgotten.

He succeeded. And those who slogged through the mud and cursed those guys up there having it so easy will have a new respect for them through his book. War is not glorified, and anyone can find out here how terrible war can be.

(October 8/October 9, 1986)

'... they helped us at great risk and saved our lives.'

The most dangerous place to hide a couple of U.S. airmen downed over France early in World War II proved to be a wine cellar. It was dangerous because there was nothing else to do there except drink wine. That caused them to sing the Air Corps song—a bad idea with Germans drinking upstairs. Luckily, it was Bastille Day, and the Germans were tipsy, too.

Insurance man Tom Hunt Sr., a 23-year-old bombardier in 1943, and nine others bailed out of their burning B-17 bomber and were hidden by French farmers. Dave Wilmot, navigator and part of the basement duet, was later captured, as were all the others except Hunt and turret gunner Bill Aguiar, who were helped across the Spanish border in a sixty-three-day odyssey.

"Our host was Ferdinand Regaine, former French intelligence officer and travel guide for Cook's Tours," Hunt said. "He had conducted tours for Presidents Coolidge and Taft, as well as for many ambassadors and celebrities. He hid six of us near where we came down. He was a very brave man who took chances to flaunt his bravery. He helped 287 men from the RAF, RCAF, and American Air Corps escape. Shortly after we left, he was captured by the Germans and sent to Buchenwald. They really worked him over; but they never killed him, because he was high up in the Resistance movement and they hoped to get information from him.

"On the train going south I broke a rule. I was supposed to stare at a magazine. I put it down and a German officer asked me a question. I nodded. He asked again. I shrugged. He got up and hurried out. Luckily the train stopped about then, and the girl following us got us all off."

Hunt returned home for pilot training and served in the Air Force for twenty-two years before retiring. Stationed in France in 1955, he located Regaine.

"In 1970 he came to the reunion of the 384th Bomb Group as our guest of honor. I took him to my hometown, Birmingham, and then to New Orleans. We stopped at Al Hirt's place. After the first show I went backstage and told Hirt's valet what M. Regaine had done. The music started with a rendition of the "Marseillaise." With the spotlight on him, Al Hirt told the audience about him and they gave him a long, standing ovation. He was very moved.

"He came to Corpus Christi and was here during [Hurricane] Celia. He said he really didn't need such a big welcome. We visited him in June and will return in May.

"He holds France's highest military decoration, equivalent to the Medal of Honor. We were seated at the rear of the Lido in Paris when a waiter saw his decoration. They carried our table almost on the stage where the showgirls flirted with him. He is ninety-three now, but his mind is as sharp as it was sixty years ago."

Hunt also located two men who were boys when they watched an aerial dogfight between Germans and Americans. They saw the P-47 piloted by Hunt's brother William shot down. They managed to get his identification and some belongings before the Germans arrived.

Their father wrote Hunt's mother a very sympathetic letter giving details of William's death and how they buried him in their village cemetery not far from where Hunt's plane crashed the year before. The Frenchman's sons described the battle and showed Hunt the grave.

"It was a very emotional meeting," Hunt said.

"When we were shot down, we were losing the war. They had nothing to gain by helping us. But they did, at great risk, and saved our lives. The French are cussed and discussed today, but those patriotic Frenchmen will always be heroes to some of us."

(February 1, 1984)

'It means there is now recognition to prisoners of war . . .'

I have known Harry Ullom for a long time. We used to talk while working out at a health club. He was teaching economics and business at Del Mar College. During all those conversations he never mentioned that he was a prisoner of war.

This week Ullom, now retired, got a medal for the experience. It is the Prisoner of War Medal, struck earlier this year. There are 142,000 living Americans who were prisoners of war back as far as World War I.

"It's merely recognition for being a prisoner of war," Ullom said. "In my case, it amounted to getting shot down. We didn't do anything heroic. Then again, we didn't do anything anti-heroic. It means there is now recognition to prisoners of war of World War I, World War II, Korea, and Vietnam. It seems that those held captive in Vietnam really brought about the recognition for all the other wars."

Korean War prisoners were seriously condemned because so many were accused of collaboration, he said. "POWs are somehow suspect. All the John Wayne, Arnold Schwarzenegger, Rambo-type movies have given the American people the perception that we should have been able to take over the camp and run our captors off or kill them and set all the other prisoners free.

"It's like we're somehow disgraced because we didn't pull out a secret weapon and win."

The medal set him to remembering the POW experience for the first time in years. He said he never joined any veterans' organization that would have revived the memory.

He started flying in October 1943 and was with the 8th Air Force as a bombardier when his B-17 was shot down near Ludwigshafen, Germany, January 7, 1944. He had flown twenty-eight missions. One of them was an attack on the IG Farben chemical plant that resulted in the largest civilian loss in all the air raids over Germany.

"The bombs released poison gas which filtered down into the

bomb shelters and killed thousands of people. That was not publicity people wanted then. Today people are more curious," he said.

On the mission on which his plane was downed, an anti-aircraft burst knocked out one engine as they approached Mansheim. Bombs were dropped. A second engine was shot out.

"Our plane straggled from the formation. We were headed for Switzerland when we were attacked by six German fighter planes, which had been waiting for crippled bombers. Then we were involved in a big aerial dogfight. An American P-38 and a P-47 shot down a German plane, and I think our gunners shot down two others. The P-47 was shot down and our third engine shot out. We went into a spin."

All managed to escape the plane, but the tail gunner's parachute failed to open. Ullom was last to get out and credits divine assistance with helping him break the centrifugal force. He hit the ball turret, injuring his knee. He was captured and sent to Stalag 1, a prison for flying officers. They fared better than most prisoners of war, likely because of orders issued by Hermann Goering, Adolf Hitler's air marshal. Food was poor, but it was the same as that the Germans were eating. Only those who attempted to escape were shot or beaten.

"Prison was one of the best things that happened to me," Ullom said. "I learned patience, self-sufficiency, and a great deal about people. Under stress, the best comes out of them."

(November 4, 1988)

'There was one hell of an explosion below.'

The B-17, trying to catch up with its squadron over Germany, nosed below the storm clouds. Suddenly an anti-aircraft shell knocked out both starboard engines. An explosion burst under the bomb bay and the plane lurched out of control. That was nearly thirty-five years ago near the village of Bellheim, Germany.

This week five of that crew held a reunion at the beach home of John D. Roberts at Port Aransas and watched a B-17 in the Confederate Air Force performance at Harlingen.

I joined the party Sunday with radioman-gunner Roberts, pilot Joe Hourtel of New Jersey, bombardier Carlos Whitehead of St. Louis, and tail gunner Don Miller of Vancouver, Washington, to hear of that nineteenth and final mission. (Ball turret gunner Sam Reeve had already returned to his home in Memphis.)

"Our plane wouldn't start and we took an alternate. We were late and were trying to catch up to our group. Weather was bad. We were to drop our bombs and land at Paris," Whitehead said.

"We were down to 9,500 feet when the shell gutted No. 3 engine and there was one hell of an explosion below," Roberts said.

"I couldn't feather the engines," Hourtel said, "and the landing gear dropped. The plane was unflyable. I rolled the trim back, cut the power, and sounded emergency."

Whitehead jettisoned the bomb load.

"I saw it land on top of a village," Miller said.

Roberts was radioing their situation to England. "I looked up and saw a church steeple go by. I didn't know how high that steeple was, but I knew we were late for supper."

"We were so low I could see the leaves on the trees when I jumped," Miller said.

"I was pulled backward, swung forward, and started the back swing when my butt hit the swamp," Roberts said.

Hourtel's chute caught in a tree and pulled from the pack. He was hurled into the soft dirt. "I sat up and saw both my legs in their fleece-lined boots floating down a stream."

His memories of the next week are blurred. Whitehead had a knife in his boot (He could have got us killed being found with a weapon, the others teased). The knife cut the parachute shrouds to provide tourniquets for the injured pilot.

Co-pilot Martin Kane died when his chute failed to open.

"Free Frenchmen on the ground shot at us as we were coming down," Miller said, but on the ground they helped. Hourtel was taken to a French hospital, then to an Army field hospital.

"The troops were the Texas 36th Division, over there since North Africa," Whitehead said. "They'd been there two months. They were using an old beer warehouse to store dead soldiers. They had five-gallon cans of schnapps, and we were soon as embalmed as the stiffs."

The men rested and rejoined another crew. "The regular crew of that plane was mad because we broke it," Whitehead said.

Hourtel now walks without a limp and still flies. He is vice president of a testing laboratory. Whitehead is with RCA. Roberts, after years with Westinghouse, has Port Aransas properties. Miller, owner of an insurance agency, returned to the site of the crash. A nephew in the Army there took him to a restaurant high on a hill.

"Say, uncle, did you know this building used to be a flak tower?"

"No kidding," Miller said. "Who'd have thought they'd put anti-aircraft around a little town like this?"

"We can laugh now," Hourtel said. "After thirty-five years officers don't get no respect. We don't relive it every Wednesday at the American Legion. But we shared something. It's great to be together again."

I left. It was their party.

(October 9, 1979)

'. . . we never had a chance to fire.'

Leo and Dan Golzman, brothers who operate Alamo Loan Co., were born into the loan business. Their father, Israel, escaped from Russia in 1920. He boarded a ship without knowing where it was going and ended up in Galveston, Texas. He took a bus as far as his money would permit and stepped off in Corpus Christi. With help from the Jewish community, he became a peddler until he could open a store and pawnshop business.

"I don't know how he did it," Leo said. "Suddenly he appears in a strange country. Doesn't understand the language. Starts supporting a family. And succeeds."

Merchandise at their store includes stereos, calculators, luggage, radios, rods and reels, and jewelry.

"What about the guns?" I asked.

Both Leo and Dan said they hate guns and no member of the family has one in the house.

"We seriously considered stopping handling them about a year ago, but it wouldn't solve anything if everyone else is still selling them."

Neither of the brothers is a stranger to guns. Dan was an infantryman in Korea. Leo was a tail gunner on a B-26 bomber over Germany.

He holds a rare distinction. He was one of the few airmen to be wounded by a rock. As his plane was landing in France, he stuck his head out of a hatch. A rock flew from the runway and hit him in the eye.

"I was in the hospital for a month," he said. "When I got out, the war was over."

Earlier, however, he had an opportunity to shoot at the world's first jet fighter, the 262 Messerschmitt.

"We weren't trained for that sort of thing," he said. "We had been taught to lead and fire, but they were gone so fast we never had a chance to fire."

(April 18, 1975)

Along with the hunger and misery, there was humor.

Tommy Worsham has one of the rarest of books. And he wrote it himself. It is a diary he kept while in Stalag Luft 3, a prisoner-of-war camp in northeast Germany for captured airmen. Such records were forbidden and could have got him shot. In very neat but dim pencil handwriting, he chronicled how his plane went down on a raid into Austria. For some reason all fighter plane protection was pulled off, and German fighters destroyed his group.

"Seven out of our crew of ten got out," he said. "That wasn't bad. Only twenty-seven out of 110 men who went down that day lived."

The diary begun a few days later recalled how the tail gunner was blown out of the plane. A 20-millimeter shell tore through the waist gunner's chest. Another blew Worsham's boot off and sent shrapnel into his leg. He was captured by armed farmers and turned over to SS troops, who beat him with a rifle butt. After time in a hospital, he was sent to the prison compound later made famous by the movie *The Great Escape*, in which many prisoners escaped, but only one or two reached safety. Fifty were caught, shot, and their bodies burned. The remains were carried back to the camp as a warning. Prisoners made a monument of dirt and a little cement to honor the victims.

"I would like to go back someday to see if it is still there," he said. "Someone was always planning an escape, and we were always thinking of diversions. We were digging a tunnel when we left.

"I bunked with some Poles. One officer had walked across Poland, Germany, and France and flown with the Royal Air Force. He was shot down and captured as British. He taught me how to survive and fathered me. When I first arrived, he told me there was another American officer in the barracks. Imagine my surprise. It was R. S. Carter. We went to Corpus Christi High School together. He used to date my sister. He went to England and I went to North Africa. We were both shot down and ended up at the same camp."

Worsham's thoughts, as reflected in the diary, were always on food. He wrote: "I promise myself never to be hungry again as long as

I'm able to do any kind of work. I don't know what starvation means, but I do know what it is to be hungry. We add lots of water in rations and it works for a while. I honestly would be satisfied with pinto beans every meal if I had a full bowl of them."

On March 13, 1945, he wrote, "The last Red Cross food was received fifteen days ago. It was four-fifths of a parcel. The last will be gone tomorrow."

German food consisted of a can of soup and a piece of bread each day. The Germans themselves had little. He and his friends played a game, listing things they would like to have. It sounded like a grocery store inventory and covered three pages. There was a similar listing for things he missed, such as toothbrushes, toilet paper, radios, cars, reading, candy, hard drinks, feminine companionship, and pages more with the conclusion, "Oh, hell. Just anything there is."

At times, Worsham said, along with the hunger and misery, there was humor, and life in the camp was a little like the TV show "Hogan's Heroes."

"There were guys in the camp who could do anything. Some could make a perfect passport. Others could sew a suit of clothes. We got materials with the help of two guards. The same guards gave warning when a search was coming up. We had a radio and listened to the news on BBC every night. They wanted that radio. But we always had it hidden, under the fireplace. A lot of the guys were expert pickpockets. When the guards came in to search, the guys would steal flashlights, knives, and all sorts of things. The guards would come back looking for the flashlights, and our guys would steal more stuff."

However, prison generally wasn't funny. Life became a nightmare when the prisoners were moved as the Russian army advanced and the Germans fled. Men sewed newspapers in their coats and between pairs of trousers for insulation against the cold. Even then most suffered frostbite in marches in temperatures that plunged to 27 degrees below zero. They marched twenty miles a day with little food. Allied bombings and strafings became more numerous, and some men were killed by our own planes.

The diary tells of residents of a bombed-out village demanding the prisoners be shot. "The Jerries thought they should do something, so they beat us with clubs."

Training from his Polish friend helped him during this period. "He taught me to save chocolate and sugar from the Red Cross packages, no matter how hungry I was," Worsham said. "On the march a little each day gave me the energy to make it. One day someone yelled my name. It was King Weldon, another Corpus Christi boy. I don't know how he recognized me. He had been an aerial gunner.

"People were helpful. The slave laborers shared their rations. Many were Poles and my friend helped me. I learned you don't freeze if you can find horses to sleep between. They won't step on you, either. We managed to steal eggs and find potato graves to rob.

"I have learned to have more regard for my fellow man. We have all learned to stick together and cooperate with one another. I've learned to be conservative, to think of the future and be prepared to ration the present for the future. I've lived by it ever since."

The prisoners were moved constantly on foot or by train. At Nuremburg many prisoners died in bombings. Reports said Hitler planned to have all the prisoners shot.

"We organized an army so we could charge the guards if we had to die. We wouldn't go like the Jews in the concentration camps. Bugs were eating us up. Fleas and lice. We burned our beds and slept on the floor."

The marches continued. The war was winding down and the prisoners found more food. Some caught frogs and ate them. The men got up a $25 pool guessing at liberation day. Worsham drew 29, a winner. They were liberated on April 29, 1945.

"At Moosburg they crowded 186 of us into a small room," he said. "We could hear explosions. One night most of the guards left. By morning they were all gone. At sunrise we saw American tanks coming over the hill. There was a lot of fighting yet, but it was over. Then we got scared. The SS fired through the camp. We hid anywhere we could.

"General Patton was standing up in the lead tank. Shiny helmet. Pearl-handled pistols. In a few minutes he was making a speech commending us for the way we had held up an army. I got to shake his hand."

In big letters across the diary was written, "WHOOPIE!!" On the next page, "Old Glory flies over Moosburg. We are going home."

(May 9/May 12, 1980)

The Final Days

Photo courtesy of R. A. Martin

The Enola Gay, the B-29 that carried the first atomic bomb dropped in warfare, on the runway on the island of Tinian

Early on the morning of August 6, forty years ago, a lone B-29 Superfortress roared down one of the long white runways on the island of Tinian, climbed to 30,000 feet, leveled off, and set a course for a place called Hiroshima. The pilot was Col. Paul Tibbets Jr., and he had named his ship the *Enola Gay* after his mother. The flight was to change the course of world history.

But at the time airmen on Tinian sort of wondered about the two B-29s that had arrived nonstop from the States, which was unusual. They noticed the bomb bay fuel tanks from the planes were bigger than any they had ever seen. And it was strange that guards were posted to keep everyone away from them.

"We were curious," said R. A. Martin, a member of the ground force at Tinian, "because the planes had been stripped down and they moved them over pits where they could keep them out of sight. We knew the planes were different, but we didn't know how.

"We had a captain in our outfit, and he kept bragging that the war was going to be over in two or three days. He was absolutely right, but we found out later he didn't know any more about the atom bombs than we did. The planes went out several times with the other B-29s on bombing raids, apparently for practice. And when the *Enola Gay* took off that morning, I don't think we paid any more attention to it than we would to any of the other planes.

"That night I was in C.Q., sitting there leaning back in my chair looking at the outdoor picture show down the way. All of a sudden there was all sorts of hollering and going on. All the men came running up and yelling, 'The war's over. The war's over. They dropped a big bomb on Hiroshima.'

"They started digging out applejack, raisin jack, and anything else they could find that had been fermented, and the celebration went on all night. C.Q. was usually duty where you could rest, but there wasn't any rest that night."

The atomic bomb must have been one of the best kept secrets, he said, because nobody on the island except the scientist who went on that flight and the colonel in charge actually knew what was going on. After the raid the *Enola Gay* was still heavily protected by a guard.

"We went over to take pictures of it, and they told us no photographs were permitted. But about then, some of the guys from the guards' outfit showed up and started taking pictures, so they didn't stop us when we went on and started taking them."

Martin—often called Ray, but that is because his initials, R. A., stand for nothing—had a small darkroom at the back of his office. When the air crewmen learned of this, they brought their pictures to be developed and he made prints for himself. He has quite a collection of pictures of the B-29s, their devastated targets, and a number of planes wrecked taking off for or returning from raids on Japan. One Superfort made it back after the bomb load of another plane fell through its tail section, nearly destroying it.

"The bombing of Japan had been going on for a long time, and from the pictures it is difficult to tell damage from conventional bombs and the atomic bombs," Martin said. "The towns burned like straw, sometimes leaving almost nothing standing."

By this time there were no fighter planes to challenge the bombers, but occasionally they returned badly shot up from ground fire, and a number of them crashed into the end of the runways, which were built up thirty or forty feet.

Martin said the Japanese seem to have been stunned. "We dropped the second one as a convincer," he said. "But I remember the first one. We celebrated it as the end of the war, which it was."

Now the anniversary of the atom bomb and what it did to people in the two Japanese cities causes a lot of remembrances and reassessments. Television images show the damage, and interviews show the human misery brought by the sudden flash from the sky that caused more destruction than any other event staged by man. A lot of the focus on the observances concerns the morality of dropping the bomb. Some would make Harry Truman out to be a monster for making the decision to use such a dreadful weapon.

Before he did it, he issued an ultimatum that Japanese Premier Suzuki said was "unworthy of public notice."

Viewpoints have a way of changing with time. Logic and hindsight come from people who were not facing an enemy who seemed happy to die rather than surrender. There were eleven million Americans in uniform at the time. I don't remember any of them feeling any guilt or remorse when we learned what had happened. We had suffered 300,000 casualties, killed and wounded, in the Pacific. Many were from kamikazes.

Our military leaders conservatively estimated we would suffer one million more casualties in an assault on the Japanese home islands, where men, women, and children were expected to die defending their homeland for the emperor.

The bomb stories are indeed terrible. A Japanese girl who survived the firebombing of Tokyo told me not long after the war how the houses, made of wood and paper, burned like gasoline. Thousands of civilians ran to the streets to escape the flames, only to die from lack of oxygen. The streets were lined with bodies stacked like cordwood six feet high for miles and miles.

These raids that had destroyed up to fifty percent of Tokyo, Osaka, and Yokohama killed more people than the bombs that fell on Hiroshima and Nagasaki. So it isn't that people in Japan weren't expecting death from the air.

We feel sympathy when individuals are counted among the casualties and we hear the survivors. But we don't comprehend deaths recorded in millions. The Japanese entered the war with 6,090,000 in their armed forces. They lost 1,210,000 killed. The Japanese killed 2.2 million Chinese, who had an army of 5 million. Russia lost 7.5 million dead out of 12.5 million in the armed forces. Germany had 3.5 million killed out of 10.2 million. Our dead were 291,000 out of 12.3 million in service.

And the dead don't even count the millions of Jews, Poles, Russians, and others the Germans gassed or shot or burned and the millions of British, Chinese, and Russian civilians who died. These numbers don't mean anything. They are just a bunch of zeroes unless you could see the bodies of everybody living in Texas and California and maybe a couple of other states heaped up in one big pile.

What strikes me in all the remembrances of the terrible bombs is the lack of mention of the lives they saved. More than 300,000 died at Hiroshima and Nagasaki. But had the Japanese fought from ditch to ditch and house to house, as Winston Churchill promised the British would do, the Japanese casualties would have run into the millions. And our own losses would have been in the vicinity of half a million dead.

I think about this, because an awful lot of good people would not have made it back to this country to attend college on the GI Bill, to get jobs, and raise families. Many among the crop of war babies who now decry the action of Harry Truman might not be here today had he not made the decision.

I think about that, because I might not be here either.

(August 5/August 6, 1985)

Jean LaFitte would have been proud of that crew . . .

Sunday was a day to remind you of invasions. In case you forgot, it was the thirty-third anniversary of the invasion of the Normandy Coast by the Allied Forces. It made Cline (Chick) Knowles give thanks for another invasion that never took place, though he and his crew were ready for it.

Jean LaFitte would have been proud of that crew—as fine a band of rascals and cutthroats as you would ever want to sail a pirate ship. Only they weren't to crew a privateer. They were to lead an invasion for the United States Navy. They were qualified in a wide variety of specialties—murder, rape, robbery, assault, burglary, sodomy, desertion, and what have you. The Navy called them "retreads."

Chick and other officers aboard six LSTs had other names for them. They represented brigs at Great Lakes, Pearl Harbor, San Diego, San Pedro, San Francisco, and a few from the Corpus Christi air training command.

Each prisoner had to be a volunteer. Prison time would be forgiven, and each would receive an "administrative discharge"—less than honorable yet with no strings attached. All they had to do was bear the brunt as the first wave in landing on the Japanese coast. The movie *The Dirty Dozen* was no fiction the way the U.S. Navy wrote the script.

"I didn't see much of a way out," Chick said. "If the Japanese didn't kill me, my own men would."

I wondered how Chick managed to land such a plum of an assignment.

"Maybe it was because of who I didn't know," he laughed. "But more likely it was because I had done some boxing at the University of Oklahoma when I was in NROTC. You see, those guys weren't ready to follow orders from anyone unless it could be backed up with fists."

There were three officers and two rated enlisted men aboard each of the six LSTs in Task Force 95. Each ship had fifty-five crewmen aboard. They referred to the vessels as "kamikaze" ships, a correct assessment.

"One of the enlisted ratings was named Bull Durham. He was covered with tattoos and had spent years in the China fleet before the war, which meant he was tough enough for the job.

"We kept all of our side arms locked up in the old man's safe. The butcher knives in the galley were kept behind very heavy mesh wire. Even tools were locked," he said. "We couldn't take any chances. You could never get a one of them to tell you why he was convicted. They all claimed to have been 'framed.' We anchored off Alcatraz Island as we prepared to leave. It was an unlikely place for them to escape to."

Of course, the explosions of the atomic bombs and the sudden surrender of Japan made the invasion unnecessary.

"So far as I know, the Navy kept its commitment to these men and released them," Chick said. "We sent them in a small group at a time. Before the process was completed, I took the submachine guns and pistols in. They were cut up with torches so no one could use them. We were relieved when the decommissioning was complete."

Chick later served in Japan and Korea. He participated in atomic bomb tests at Eniwetok and later took pilot training. He was at the Corpus Christi Naval Air Station when he retired in 1966 after twenty-four years of service.

He is well into his second career as a high school teacher. Sometimes pressure builds up at school, but it is nothing compared to the "Dirty Dozen" invasion that never came off.

(June 7, 1977)

A Different Kind of War

The crew of Huckins PT 259 on Midway Island in 1944. The author is standing fourth from the right. (Above) The 259 on a training mission in the Hawaiian Islands in 1944

Pearl Harbor tends to make World War II veterans nostalgic, because that was the event that altered their lives. From the minute we heard the broadcast after lunch in the orphanage that December Sunday, we knew our future had been determined.

The first one to speak after the announcement said, "At least we won't have to look for a job when we graduate."

In the orphanage I grew up with the same philosophy they used in the service: "Don't ever volunteer for anything." However, I couldn't volunteer for the service when I graduated from high school in 1943 because the government had put a temporary freeze on enlistees younger than eighteen. So I registered for the draft and was ordered by Draft Board No. 1, Waxahachie, Texas, to report to Dallas for a physical examination and induction into the service.

There were about thirty of us, mostly farm boys from Central Texas. A number were rejected for physical defects, including a muscular fellow who was missing a toe from a threshing machine accident. At 6 feet, 2 inches, 120 pounds, I was in great shape.

The final lineup was to assign us to various armed services. They grumbled and groaned as clerks announced the assignments. The farm boys were not happy when they found they were headed for the Navy. They didn't trust water. I wanted Navy.

The clerk told me, "You're the first one all day who's got what he wanted."

Then he stopped, put his hand on my shoulder, and told the two behind me, the last two in line, "You men are in the Marine Corps."

(December 9, 1986/December 18, 2009)

... wild times with George Bush

Joe O'Brien, known as a spokesman for the Corpus Christi Taxpayers Association, recalls the "wild" times he had with President-elect George Bush when they were Navy flight cadets together in 1942.

"We were in pre-flight training at the University of North Carolina. We could go into town at Chapel Hill on weekends. We would get to town at 1 p.m. after lunch, take in a movie, have a milkshake, then go to the other theater in town for a second movie, and go back to the campus. There was nothing else to do. We had to be in by 10 p.m.

"That was our wild weekend in Chapel Hill. There wasn't anything to get into. According to the regulations, we couldn't walk down the street holding hands with a girl. We couldn't sit in a car.

"They held dances on Saturday nights, but one of the requirements for entry was you had to take off your shoes. This was supposed to be to save the gymnasium floor. But they were keeping us away from the college girls, because we would be out of uniform without shoes.

"I met George Bush on August 4, 1942, when he got on the train at either New Haven or Stamford, Connecticut," O'Brien said. "I got on the train for North Carolina at Pawtucket, Rhode Island.

"We were enrolled in the V-5 Navy flight training program. We started as apprentice seamen at $52 a month. But after two weeks of active duty, the president signed a law and we became cadets and our pay increased to $75 a month.

"George and I were in the same platoon. He was in Room 34 and I was in Room 316 in Lewis Hall. Every now and then the training officer of the platoon behind us took charge of us. That ensign would end up chewing me out every time. His name was Jerry Ford," O'Brien said, referring to the former president.

"Jerry came in as an athletic training officer. Every Saturday they sent us on long marches. Once we reached a lake and they let us lay around for half an hour, which was unusual.

"Then they told us we were going to set a new record in running the eight miles back to the campus. I was determined that if George could make it, I could, too. He later told me he wasn't going to quit if I didn't drop out. Out of the whole battalion only three guys dropped out. We set a new record. Jerry Ford ran beside us the whole way.

"As a reward for setting the record, they let us stay in town an extra thirty minutes. We didn't have to be back in our rooms until 10:30. What a reward!

"We were at Chapel Hill three months, studying mathematics, navigation, Morse code, ship identification, and academic and military subjects.

"While we were there, Barbara came down to visit George. I carried her bags so George could devote his whole attention to her. The thing I remember about her was the quality of her face. It's a quality that shows through after all those years. George had a baby face. He looked really young. He still looks very young for his age."

O'Brien said he has met Bush at various political gatherings through the years and Bush recognized him.

"After he gave a speech here several years ago, I told him, 'I don't remember you talking like that forty years ago.'

"He said, 'Forty years ago I couldn't even talk.'"

O'Brien got his flight training at Pensacola, Florida, and ferried planes from the factory to the West Coast.

Bush became a combat pilot in the Pacific, was shot down, and rescued by an American submarine.

Gerald Ford also served in the Pacific on an aircraft carrier and was discharged as a lieutenant commander.

"Just think, I used to eat three meals with George Bush," O'Brien said, "and the government was paying for it. Now I guess I'd have to pay to eat with George."

(December 15, 1988)

... a Herman Melville introduction to the seagoing life

For good reason, a tanker passing under Harbor Bridge made me think of my first ocean voyage. It was on a tanker. We were fresh out of boot camp. We didn't know where we were going when they ordered us aboard a truck at the receiving station on Terminal Island at San Pedro, California, and headed for the harbor. We had no idea what kind of ship we were headed for or what kind of duty we would get.

I thought I had been assigned to radar school. But this didn't look like it. We pulled up alongside a ship that looked like a tanker. It was painted Navy gray and it had four five-inch guns and quite a few anti-aircraft guns—much more armament than you would expect on a tanker. As we unloaded our gear, we noticed that Shore Patrolmen lined the dock—about twenty of them. We tried to figure out what was so valuable that would require that many guards.

We climbed the gangplank and were greeted by a surly boatswain who ordered us to an empty cabin where we stowed our gear. Only a few crewmen were about. Their hair was shorter than ours. Our boot camp haircuts were growing out, but these guys' heads were shaved. Nobody seemed anxious to talk. We went back on deck to see what was going on. There were even more guards on the dock now.

Then a couple of trucks drove up filled with sailors in dungarees and almost an equal number of SPs carrying rifles. The sailors reluctantly boarded the ship with guards right behind them. They were quickly hustled below. This was repeated several times, and the dock was practically covered with SPs. Then the ship started its engines, the deck crew cast off lines, and just before dark we headed out to sea.

It didn't take long to learn that this was not a happy ship. You could tell the passengers from the crew. All the latter had shaved heads. The captain came on the speaker. His voice was angry and threatening. He announced a number of strict rules and punishment that would be administered to violators. We were sent to the boiler room to receive our orders. The roar was deafening. I never did hear what the chief yelled at us. I followed the other guys to a 40-millimeter gun station.

There we began to learn about the ship, the USS *Cimarron*. It had accompanied the carrier *Hornet* carrying the B-25 bombers under Gen. Jimmy Doolittle that conducted a surprise raid on the Japanese mainland on April 18, 1942.

Before the planes were launched, the *Cimarron* fueled the fleet. After the launch the fleet quickly retreated at flank speed—thirty-five knots. The *Cimarron*, with a top speed of twenty-six knots, was left alone off the coast of Japan, full of explosive fumes and with no protection at all.

Fortunately, the Japanese had no idea the planes were launched from a carrier, and the tanker eventually returned to the States unharmed. But the crew members felt they had been deceived into taking part in a suicide mission. Many went over the hill as soon as the ship got home. The SPs managed to round up some of them. The rest of the complement was filled with prisoners from the brig. The captain was given this command as punishment for running a destroyer aground. He was determined to make somebody pay, and the crew was ripe for whipping. We had boarded a hell ship. Everyone snarled at one another.

On lookout duty some other passenger said something funny, and I laughed. Nobody else was laughing on that ship. My good humor got me a job with real depth. I was sent down a narrow shaft to the very bottom of the ship where I scooped up buckets of stinking, oily water from the bilges and sent it up to a fellow passenger, who stood on deck and pulled each bucket up with a line to that pinhole of light way up there on deck. We worked for hours. I was covered with oil and grime like a coal miner. The salt-water shower wasn't too efficient in removing it.

I didn't smile again for the six days it took to sail to Pearl Harbor. I was never so happy to leave a ship. It was sort of a Herman Melville introduction to the seagoing life.

Every now and then somebody mentions cruises on freighters or tankers. I watched that tanker move up channel. Naw. I wouldn't be interested in such a cruise. I've been a passenger on a tanker.

(May 25, 1987)

I really didn't have any classified information.

Remember the days when people used to have beautiful penmanship?

I don't. It must have been before my time. I'm glad, too, for my penmanship would have driven a teacher of all that neatness and clarity up the wall. It started back there in the first grade with the ovals and the pushpulls. I knew I was in trouble when my ovals kept looking like pushpulls. I never could master that muscular control, using the wrist and arm in a fluid rolling motion. As a result my handwriting never progressed beyond the wavy lines similar to those of an electrocardiogram. I was always resigned to getting D's in penmanship. Even a D didn't look too bad. I also got used to getting bad grades on essays because English teachers could never quite figure out what I was saying.

When it came to taking shorthand, I figured the quality of the squiggles didn't make all that much difference because shorthand looks like a bunch of scratching anyway. I was wrong. I found shorthand easy and pleasant to write but impossible to read.

In the Navy I was ahead of my mates in electronics school. I scribbled my notes in shorthand while they labored in longhand to get their class notebooks together. The school was a four-week course, and every day we added pages and pages to the notebook.

We were practically locked up during the course. The school was confining, and all the inmates were glad to get out. When we were checking out, the instructor checked notebooks as we went by to make certain no classified information got out. The commander did a double take over my notebook.

"What is that?" he asked.

"My notebook, sir," I explained. "It's shorthand, sir. But you don't need to worry. I can't read it and I don't think anybody else can either."

"You'd better go over it with the yeoman. We can't take any chances."

"Can't you just keep the book, sir? I have no use for it."

"You must take the book with you, but it must be cleared for security."

The yeoman wasn't happy about it either. He really wasn't happy about it when he looked at the book. "What kind of shorthand is this? I've never seen shorthand like this before. What is it?"

"Gregg," I said.

"In what language?" he asked.

He threw his hat down. The yeoman and I got pretty well acquainted over the next four days as I tried to figure out shorthand brief forms I had devised in the radar lectures. The yeoman was a surly fellow. He was also desperate. We hadn't covered half the book, and I was costing him some time on the town. In a couple of days he had to get ready for a new class.

I don't know why he didn't believe me. I really didn't have any secret or classified information in my book. I really didn't understand enough of what the MIT professor was telling us to grasp any secrets.

It hit the yeoman for the first time. "Of course," he said, "you're too stupid to have any classified information. I know for a fact you can't take shorthand. I'm going to approve your notebook, but don't you tell anyone I didn't read it all."

His secret was safe with me. And I haven't tried to take any notes in shorthand since.

(September 23, 1975)

The mine glowed red and sank.

The United States Navy looking for a minesweeper reminds me of a bunch of billionaires standing around trying to rake up a quarter so they can make a telephone call. It seems logical when a run-of-the-mill missile cruiser costs almost a billion dollars that they would want a little old minesweeper to clear out the explosives some "freedom fighter" in a canoe has planted out there.

When the tankers started running over them, we tried to borrow a minesweeper from all of our allies, but they said no. One of the earlier excuses for no minesweepers was that the hulls are made of wood and we didn't have that kind of shipyard.

I have a suspicion that if someone could locate some plans and wave about million-dollar bills, they could be building them at almost any coastal city. Helicopters with sensors have been looking for mines, but somehow the fellows in the boiler rooms of the tankers don't seem real happy about that.

I remember when the Navy had a bunch of minesweepers. I got traveling orders at Pearl Harbor, and a guy in the communications tower sent a blinker message to a passing PT Boat to pull in and pick me up. They weren't real happy about that, because I was not being assigned to their squadron and would be relief for somebody else.

They didn't pull into the landing. They tied up alongside a minesweeper. There were eight or ten other minesweepers between the dock where I was standing and the one they were moored to. In between obscenities, they were yelling for me to hurry up. I was still almost a boot but had never had that many people yelling at me all at one time. I was carrying a seabag, mattress, and hammock, which was fairly heavy but mostly bulky; and for a skinny, 125-pound kid, it was awkward throwing it from one ship to the other, then jumping a four- or five-foot gap between ships.

A minesweeper has more cables and obstructions than anything I have seen. I imagine the guys who served on them had a lot of bruises walking on deck at night. I was picking up my gear and throwing it over stuff to get to the edge so I could cross to the next ship.

It was like an obstacle course. It was hot and the crew of the boat were getting angrier and angrier. Two months later I would have taken my own good time and let them yell, but I had a lot to learn. By the time I got to the last boat, I was so tired I nearly threw my stuff in the water. I was about ready to cry. That's why I know we once had a bunch of minesweepers, and that was only one port.

As for mines, once one popped up, and we were sent to sink it. I was called out of a sound sleep and couldn't find my shoes. When I fired the bow 20-millimeter cannon, the hot shells bounced off my feet, giving me some blisters and playing the devil with my aim. The executive officer at the wheel nudged the boat forward. We had two sets of .50-caliber machine guns and my cannon firing. Now we were about thirty feet from the barnacle-encrusted mine. It looked mean, with moss on the trigger horns.

Now as I fired, I was shooting over it. I couldn't depress enough to hit it. The Exec thought I was deliberately firing high since I could almost touch the monster. Then a .50-caliber tracer hit it solid. It glowed red and sank. It didn't go poof! If it had, we would have gone with it.

I got an F for marksmanship and a great big respect for mines and minesweepers. I think the Navy ought to have a bunch of them. Of course, with red faces, the brass hats have already decided that.

(August 26, 1987)

'Last-in-line' ploy
didn't always work.

Growing up in an orphanage was in many respects like growing up in boot camp. One of the things I learned was that being last in line can help you avoid work details. At the orphanage we had regular chores, assigned during roll call. I learned to wait until assignments were made in one group. Then I would sidle over behind them until work details were assigned in my group.

Most of the time this ploy worked well in the Navy. It didn't work too well when a chief petty officer rousted us out of the sack for a docking party or such. When press gangs go to that much trouble, there is no escape.

We "volunteered" for unloading and docking parties. Neither was a party. The first involved moving cargo. It was sometimes a hot, tough job, lifting, carrying, and stacking.

Once we were unloading cases of canned goods from a Navy transport. A case of canned boned chicken broke. A couple of our crewmen grabbed a No. 10 can and hid it behind a piling. Later the rest of us allowed as how were going to have a feast on that canned chicken as a substitute for Spam. Bernie the motor mech disputed that. He and two other guys had stolen the can, and it was all theirs.

The chow was unusually bad the next day, and Bernie and his friends opened their canned chicken and made a big show of heating it up in the galley. They made a bigger show of eating every bit of it. The rest of the guys cussed them, but it didn't faze them a bit. Not until the next morning, it didn't. Then they learned the can was tainted.

All three chicken thieves got terribly sick. The guys wouldn't let them use the head in the forward crew's quarters. They had to use the aft bathroom, where it was hot and close, which made them sicker. And they had to line up to use it. That was the only time I ever saw an illness that drew cheers.

A line-handling party was assembled by pointing fingers, too. The chief boatswain commandeered a dozen or so of us who happened to be wandering around when he passed.

A carrier was to be docked, and we were to grab the big lines to make them secure. This was at Pearl Harbor in 1943. The chief climbed a cluster of pilings to oversee the operation.

Ordinarily ships docking without tugs would bring the bow close to the dock, where lines were secure. Then the stern was swung to dockside. Some of the captains were expert. Some needed two or three passes.

This time the carrier came in and kept coming. It was going too fast. The bow crunched into the piling cluster, tossing the chief about fifteen feet out into water still oily from ships sunk by the December 7 attack. The old chief came up mad as only a chief boatswain's mate can get mad. He had a beautiful vocabulary of profanity. He climbed up to the dock, yelling and waving his fist at the carrier bridge.

"What in the bleep, bleep did you think you were driving, a bleepedly bleep taxicab?"

Way up on the bridge a figure with the gold braid of an admiral looked down. He was seeing if he could still dock a big ship. He couldn't. The chief had a couple more choice comments before the admiral waved and yelled, "Sorry, chief."

The chief was a little abashed himself. He never recruited our area for another line-handling party.

And my strategy of what the Army guys called goldbricking backfired when I was sent to firefighting school. This happened not once but three times. Every time I was transferred, I ended up going to firefighting school. And every time the same thing happened.

We were standing around a realistic mockup of a ship's boiler room, where a roaring fire could be created. The instructor looked us over. He spotted me hiding in the back row.

"Hey, you. Skinny guy, there in the back. Come here."

He handed me an applicator, a long pipe with a spray nozzle attached to a fire hose. Other guys grabbed the hose behind me. The instructor explained that the thing I was holding was a fog nozzle. If I aimed the spray at the fire, it would be controlled. He emphasized that an uncontrolled fire aboard ship can quickly become catastrophe. He was right, of course, but I still couldn't see how a thin spray of fog could beat back a roaring inferno.

"Just don't let the fire get behind you. If you do, you'll be in trouble," he said.

This seemed to mean we'd have to run like blue blazes. But I didn't have time to mull this over. They set the place on fire. It was an inferno. They turned on the water and I led the group in. My companions didn't seem to have any more confidence in my ability than I did.

But remarkably the conflagration calmed down. The spray of water tamed the flames that flared up from the grated deck. They almost got behind us, but we whipped them down.

The exercise was to teach us to fight fires aboard ship and, more importantly, not to fear the flames as long as we had the equipment to control them. It was a valuable lesson that calmed our fear of the fire. After this happened to me three times, I began to feel something of an expert, but I'm very glad I never had to fight a real fire aboard ship.

The Navy always had powerful portable pumps, called "handy billies," using the sea as a source of water. Naturally, aboard ship you have to feed the hoses through hatches, around corners, and through tight places. This requires manpower, sailors spaced out feeding the hose through the maze that is a ship's innards.

Firefighting techniques have changed considerably in the years since I was exposed to them. Foam and newer methods help tackle shipboard fires.

My firefighting experience is scarcely worth a second thought, except for the guys who put us through the training. I got to know some of them. Sadly, they all died fighting a ship fire at Pearl Harbor in 1944 when LSTs preparing for the Saipan invasion, loaded with fuel and ammunition, exploded, a disaster not reported because of wartime secrecy.

Tragically, it was a small fire that could not be controlled.

(September 6, 1983)

'... you ever hear of Hogan's goat?'

He was a throwback to an earlier era. He was in charge of the sail loft, a position you wouldn't expect to find in a modern navy. I don't know how old he was.

In earlier days rhe Navy enlisted teenagers, so he was probably very young when he enlisted on what were known as baby cruises. It occurred to me he was too old to be in the Navy, but they probably would never have found another man of his seagoing knowledge. And his language was salty enough to have come from the age of sail.

Three squadrons of PT Boats were stationed at Pearl Harbor early in 1943, and his services were welcomed among the wooden boats. His tiny office at the end of the dock was crowded with the tools of his trade. There were hemp anchor lines, mooring lines, fenders to be braided and spliced, and base supplies, tools, paints, and all sorts of backup supplies.

I liked to listen to his sea stories. He spoke of the Philippine Insurrection in which the United States helped crush the Moros. "They charged with big knives," he said. "We'd empty a .45 clip into them and they kept coming. They'd drop dead at our feet."

I hadn't told him where I was from.

"You're from Texas, aren't you?" he said. I asked how he could tell.

"You said, 'Ittie bittie ol.' Only Texans say that. Southerners say 'Little bittie.' But not like you said."

One day he asked me, "Say, did you ever hear of Hogan's goat?"

I said I hadn't.

Apparently Hogan's goat was a smelly subject often used in the Old Navy: "Smelled like Hogan's goat. Was as mean as Hogan's goat. As lazy as Hogan's goat."

Hogan had a blacksmith's shop in the old Philadelphia Navy Yard. The goat roamed over the base, rooting in pigpens and eating smelly tin cans. He could always be located by a terrible smell, so anything that carried a repulsive smell was credited to the goat.

I had never heard of Hogan's goat. Made me wonder if it was an enlisted men's plot to take a jab at the goat, which happens to be the mascot of the U.S. Naval Academy football team. But that might take away from the old chief's story.

(October 23, 2009)

'... they were talking about boats, I was talking about fires.'

One of former Fire Chief John Carlisle's old American Legion buddies wrote to suggest I talk to John and ask him about how he became a Coast Guard skipper. Funny story, he said. I know it's a funny one because I've heard him tell it several times. The re-telling doesn't hurt it a bit.

In 1942 John went to an interview with the Coast Guard, where he thought his experience at fighting fires on ships might be a plus.

"They asked me the difference in a 100-footer and a 6-bitter," John says. He replied there was a difference in handling. You must compensate for the difference in weight. They asked if he had ever been aboard a tanker or freighter. He had. How long had he been around the water? All his life. They asked about his salvage experience. Yes, he had that.

"All the time they were talking about boats, I was talking about fires. They asked if I had any experience on small draft. I said 'yes,' thinking about rowboats. They were thinking 12-footers."

He was enlisted as a chief petty officer and assigned to Number 7201 at Mobile, Alabama. This was not a building, he discovered, but a patrol craft. And he was its captain.

The first class petty officer in charge was not happy to see a "slick arm" or a chief with no service stripes on his arm. He asked the new skipper if he wanted to take 'er out. John told him to do it, he wanted to check his proficiency. He asked John to drop the spring line. John didn't know what one was, so he said he was no deck hand. One of the deck hands performed the task.

First Class asked the new chief if he planned to sleep up forward with the crew. John asked where he slept. He said in the captain's quarters. That was good enough for John. He told First Class he'd have to move.

John inspected the vessel as if he knew what he was doing. The motor mech apologized for the grease in his engine room. John told him not to let it happen again. A crewman muttered the new chief was tough, but he seemed like he knew what he was doing. Then First Class was transferred.

"I told the crew I wanted each of them to learn every job on the boat and do all the chores. I stood by and watched. They didn't know I was learning, too. Pretty soon I was handling the boat pretty good."

He ran into trouble when he was told he needed fenders (the cushions between ship and pier), and the salty old chief warrant at the sail loft snarled at him to make his own. He didn't like recruit chiefs. Carlisle bought line at a hardware store and at a used book store bought a book on tying knots. He practiced tying knots all weekend at his apartment ashore.

"Monday I sent the crew to the sail loft for materials. I showed them how to braid the line over a length of hawser. Then we built a suitcase-type fender like the old book illustrated. The chief warrant came by and took a long look at the fender hanging between the hull and the dock.

"'Chief, I'm sorry I didn't have any confidence in you. I thought you were another slick arm trying to take over. But my dad was a seafaring man, and he was the only sailor I ever saw who could make a suitcase fender like that. You must come from a seafaring family.'

"I just smiled at him. Me and that warrant got along fine after that."

The moral of that might be: Once you learn the ropes, you'll be okay.

(August 28, 1985)

The huge wave
of our wake
caught the admiral's barge.

Every year about this time I get a lot of information from a group of ex-PT Boat sailors who promote a yearly convention and are working to build a Motor Torpedo Boat Museum. Most attendees are grizzled veterans, many survivors of the Solomons, the Marshalls, the Philippines, the Mediterranean, and a dozen other places. They were the "Expendables," whisking MacArthur off Corrigidor, dashing out of the darkness of Guadalcanal to do battle with the Japanese Fleet, chasing German E-Boats.

They have war stories to tell about their exploits in motor torpedo boats. People in my squadron never got to tell any of those salty war stories. McHale of the comic television PT battles didn't appear in this tragicomedy, but he could have been looking over the shoulder of MTB Ron 26 in Hawaii.

One incident occurred on a quiet Sunday afternoon early in 1944 while we were lazing around on deck at the former Pearl City Yacht Club. There were occasional whoops from up in officers' country, where a real native luau was in progress. Real stateside American whiskey was flowing—for officers only.

Suddenly we were almost pushed to the deck by the force of an explosion. It was like Pearl Harbor had been attacked all over again. A big fireball rose over the port, and exploding ammunition made brilliant streaks through the black smoke clouds.

Somehow, through accident or sabotage, two or three LSTs, fully loaded with fuel, ammunition, and materiel for an imminent invasion, suddenly exploded. I learned later that 163 men were killed. It was not reported at the time. Things like that didn't make good news at home.

Then a couple of ensigns came running down the dock and jumped aboard two boats. They ordered the engines started. Since no other brass came down the path, it was obvious these were the soberest two.

That didn't count for much. The first one tried to get under way before the three Packard Marines had warmed up and blew pistons through the overhead.

The ensign who now skippered our boat managed better. We were to stand by to torpedo the ships if they broke their moorings and endangered other ships. The ensign asked by radio how deep to set the torpedoes and security yelled him off the air.

Then he pushed all throttles forward full, and the old Nine Boat fairly leaped out of the water. A PT kicking up about fifty knots also kicks up a tremendous wake in the calm waters of a harbor.

Pearl Harbor was moving by us at a blur when all of a sudden right in front of us appeared an admiral's barge. You could tell it was an admiral's barge by the four little gold stars on a blue background. Even our party-boy ensign didn't miss that little flag. He pulled all three throttles to full stop.

We roared past the admiral's barge and stopped. Then the huge wave of our wake caught the barge. Its bottom was bright red and extremely well cared for. Then it rocked the other way and almost capsized again. It was still rocking violently this way and that when a silver haired gentleman with an extremely red, angry face became visible beside his flag.

I've heard that Adm. Chester Nimitz didn't swear. But I wouldn't swear to it. He was waving his fists and shouting.

" ... if you don't get that ... out of here, I personally will ..."

Our ensign was stone cold sober now and had the boat turned around and headed back to the Pearl City Yacht Club. The admiral was still standing, waving his fists. If they needed any torpedoes, they probably called a submarine.

The trip back was the slowest that boat ever made. I never saw that ensign again. Luckily, he was a millionaire already. He probably wouldn't have liked the Navy as a career anyway. And he probably never tells this story when PT sailors get together to swap war stories.

(December 9, 1986/December 18, 2009)

Big Willie was not a good advertisement for a college education.

Big Willie was old. He must have been almost thirty. He hadn't been away from his Oklahoma farm much before he joined the Navy. He was called "Big Willie" because his name was Williams, but there was another guy in the crew also named Williams. He was a lot bigger than Big Willie, but he was only twenty years old.

"I'll bet you one thing," Big Willie used to say with conviction. "I'm going to be the first guy in this outfit to go home."

Nobody believed him, but we humored him. Not many people were going back to the States in 1943.

Willie was an expert torpedoman. He was always taking his torpedoes apart, cleaning, oiling, and carefully reassembling them without anybody telling him to do it. He didn't join the crowds going to town on liberty. He stayed aboard the boat. He spent hours and hours sitting in his bunk writing letters. He'd stare off into space for a long time before he'd go back to writing again. If he wasn't writing, he was back taking the covers off the torpedoes, checking their innards.

I talked to Willie quite a bit. All he wanted to do was get back to his wife and his farm.

"You seem smart enough to me," he used to say. "If you're as smart as I think you are, you'll go to college when this war is over. College is a wonderful thing."

Then he told me why. His father was half Indian and had no education. Willie only got to the seventh grade when he had to quit school and go to work. He knew machinery from having worked with it all his life, but he regretted not having an education.

Maybe, I thought, that's why he labored so long and hard over those letters. It was a struggle for him, but he stayed with it. I wondered what he could write about. There wasn't much I could say in a letter because the censors wouldn't let you say where you were or where you'd been or what you were doing. Whatever he was saying, his wife must have been happy. Probably spent half her time reading letters.

"Not going to be long now," Big Willie announced one day. "I'm going to be on my way home pretty soon."

Everyone laughed and razzed him. But he just smiled and nodded.

"You'll see. Anyone want to put up any money on the first guy on this boat to go stateside?"

Nobody did. It was ridiculous. The outfit had only been overseas six months, and here was Willie saying he was going home. A lot of the other guys wished they could, too, but they didn't have any hope. Then one day an officer came running aboard, all out of breath.

"Williams, pack your gear. You are going to New London. Your orders are being cut now. You are flying back, Priority One."

I think Big Willie must have had most of his stuff already packed. It didn't take him long. He had a big smile on his face.

"Told you guys I'd be the first."

Naturally everyone wanted to know how he managed to swing it.

"Been playing with this idea ever since I was in torpedo school. Must have made a thousand sketches with notes. It's an idea for a new type turbine-driven torpedo. I sent my idea in, and they're going to let me work on it in the laboratory in New London. See you guys."

He hoisted his seabag and was gone. We never saw him again. I assume his war was in the laboratory working with highly educated scientists, helping to shorten the war for the rest of us. In spite of his advice, Big Willie wasn't a very good advertisement for a college education.

(November 7, 1977)

The big operator
was soon eating
home cooking . . .

With no tales of combat excitement to tell, we of Ron 26 had to make do with stories of liberties on other islands and escapades of swab jockeys suddenly turned loose on a lot of bad booze with too little time to drink it. One often told story involved a base force motor mechanic who was the shrewd operator. He was along when our boat made a depth-charge run. The explosions stunned and killed a lot of fish. Our passenger got permission to scoop up a couple of baskets of stunned fish.

Islanders weren't permitted to fish and were starved for them. He took a basket of the catch and made one of the sharpest bargains of his career. There were very few available women on the island. But the big operator was soon eating home cooking and having other domestic privileges from a Polynesian widow not two blocks from our base.

He was so proud of his accomplishment he never missed a chance to brag on his good fortune to us guys who had not had a handshaking acquaintance with a female in more than a year. He'd either give you a knowing leer or feign a little exaggerated nonchalance to let you know there was nothing to it. All discussions centered on how long it would take before someone cracked up and caved his skull in. All agreed the assassin should get a reward.

His domestic life continued as he courted with cigarettes and rations filched from the officers' mess. His lady love was a good fifteen years older than the motor mech and not too pretty, but he didn't mind. After all, the rest of us had to make do with Petty Girl pinups. We hated it when he came back to the base whistling too loudly.

One afternoon he came down the road with a funny walk. He staggered like he had too much green island gin. As he got closer, we could see he was covered with blood. He was slashed clear across his abdomen. He held the huge gash together with his hands. A pharmacist's mate gave him first aid.

As he waited for the doctor, he said, "I had a few drinks and went over to the house. Mona wasn't home, but her sixteen-year-old daughter was. I never saw her before. Jeez! She's a looker. Really built. She could pass for nineteen any time. I was making pretty good time with her when Mona came running in. I've never seen her that mad before. She threw her groceries on the floor. She started screaming and throwing stuff at me. She chased me all over the house. I just about made it when I looked around. She swung this big machete. I jumped back, but she cut me."

He started crying. He thought he was dying. We felt sorry for him. He was hurt, and like the rest of us, he didn't have a girl. He wasn't seriously injured. He soon healed, but he had a tremendous scar, which I am sure by now is an honored war wound. But the motor mech never did any more bragging about women. Every time he thought about them, he started getting a stomachache.

Some of the guys thought about trying to strike up an acquaintance with Mona. Some even thought about trying to make contact with her voluptuous young daughter. Then they thought about that three-foot razor blade and turned back to their Petty Girls.

War really was hell.

(March 23, 1981)

The 'Big Island'
was a real paradise.

One look at a travel folder of Hawaii and I could almost believe the myth. There were clean beaches, deep blue water, towering mountains, green vegetation topped by palms. I remembered it without the high-rise condominiums and girls in grass skirts offering fancy coconut drinks.

Compared to Oahu in 1943, where thousands of servicemen stepped on each other's toes, Hawaii, "the Big Island," was a real paradise. We got a week's liberty there before shipping out. Hilo Harbor was empty except for our boats. We appeared to have the whole town to ourselves.

My older shipmates were showing me the ropes, and we settled in a nice little bar. It was a dramatic moment, for I was about to sample my very first cocktail. We were served by a very polite Japanese man. We had only a couple of sips when a bunch of ragged Marines came in, completely out of uniform. One of them pulled a trench knife and threw it into a post—not an inch above the waiter's head.

"Drinks are on the house," he yelled and jumped the bar. We looked up and saw a couple of military police and shore patrol racing down the street. We bailed out of a restroom window before a war started in there.

A little later we retreated to a restaurant. They couldn't export beef then. A platter-sized T-bone was a dollar. A soldier and his girlfriend were sitting nearby with a table filled with food. Two Marines came in, grabbed the soldier's table, and flipped it and the food upside down. Almost immediately SPs and MPs appeared and fired .45 pistols over our heads at the fleeing Marines.

Still later we found rooms at a hotel and started a party. Some Marines joined in, and we began to get an idea of what they were angry at. They were assault troops in the Tarawa invasion. Someone goofed and didn't figure the tides. Men were dumped off in fifteen feet of water, many of them with machine guns or other heavy equipment strapped to them. Losses were heavy, and the survivors came back with what clothes they had on their backs.

They looked for girls in Hawaii. Army troops stationed there two years had the girls. So the Marines took out their anger on the Army. I was glad they weren't mad at us.

The party continued late. Most of the Marines passed out. The night manager came up to complain. Someone gave him a drink, and he joined the party. He was soon snoozing in a corner.

Then Little Willie, a tall, good-looking guy from Kentucky, made a remark about his prowess with all of Northern womankind.

Hagerty, a hot-tempered Boston Irishman, retorted that his mother was from the North and furthermore Little Willie was a no-good Rebel obscenity.

That's when Willie smashed a gin bottle and prepared to groove Hagerty's face. I grabbed Willie from behind, and somebody made the big move to knock him out. It didn't work. The fist caught my chin and knocked me over a bed and out.

The next morning we called a cab. But the driver didn't take us to the boat. He went to police headquarters. We were dirty, sick, and bloody from a cut on Willie's hand. Somebody had stolen twenty cases of Five-Island Gin. And, although we had paid $12 a bottle for the five-day-old poison, we looked like prime suspects. We were sick and in trouble. They wouldn't give us a drink of water. No aspirin. We were dying. After several painful hours our officers rescued us. But we couldn't go ashore again.

I don't think I would want to go back. With all those high rises and all, it just wouldn't be the same.

(May 8, 1980)

'... whatever Jones did, the captain never did anything to him.'

One of my favorite sea stories comes from Russell Beardsley, the former crewman who was so upset over the sale of the cruiser *Phoenix* to Argentina. He told me about the ship's scrounger, an old salt named Jones, who was the equivalent of Luther Billis, the wheeler-dealer in *Tales of the South Pacific*.

"Jones was about 5-foot-9, had reddish hair, and was maybe forty years old. He had been in the Navy twenty-three years and was still a seaman second class, the lowest rank possible outside of boot camp. He was the sloppiest sailor in the United States Navy," Beardsley said.

"He was satisfied as the lowest rank aboard. He was happy. He didn't have any responsibility, and they couldn't bust him because he didn't have any stripes to lose. [Newspaper columnist] Walter Winchell once wrote a paragraph about Jones' low rank.

"Jones had the ship's gambling concession. One sailor won a lot of money. Jones went ashore to beat the sailor up and take his money. It didn't work. The sailor beat Jones up good and took his money—a big roll of it.

"I don't know why it was but whatever Jones did, the captain never did anything to him. There wasn't much he could do. Jones was always restricted to the ship anyway. He could have put him in the brig, but the ship would have run short on services. He ran the haircut concession. He would get your whites pressed for a quarter.

"Jones also ran an after-hours gedunk stand. You could go down and get ice cream or candy any time after ships service closed, at Jones' price. He was always saying, 'I wired a thousand dollars home' or 'I wired two thousand dollars home this week.'

"Some of the things he did were crazy. Remember the shipboard heads?"

I remembered the long trough with a single board running the length of it. Under it was a continuous rush of salt water. It was an open community toilet and no place for the bashful.

"Jones soaked some paper in polish, put it in a lid, and set it on fire. It flared up and he sent it down the way, singeing two ensigns who were sitting on the board."

This alone was enough to make him a hero to the crew.

"Once he showed up for inspection wearing a pair of dirty shorts and a T-shirt. The captain told him to go below. Another time we were standing in ranks and he was fishing behind him with a hand line. As the captain came by, he caught a fish. The captain said, 'Pull in your fish, Jones.'

"Jones always managed to get ashore one way or another. One day he went down the bowline. When he came back that night, the tide was in and the line was nearly straight up. He climbed up to the rat guard and couldn't get up or down. It was cold and he had four bottles of booze under his pea coat. He started screaming. He fell into the water and nearly drowned before they fished him out.

"Jones got caught trying to bring an Australian girl aboard in a sea bag. I don't know how he planned to use her."

Beardsley was busted to seaman second when he was caught gambling on Jones' roulette wheel.

"Jones was already seaman deuce," Beardsley said. "He wasn't worried. But he always wore a full money belt and a life preserver. He wasn't so much afraid of drowning as he was of going down with all that money."

Jones is probably very old if he's still alive and likely very rich.

(May 18, 1982)

... the sickest, most miserable PT sailor in history

You had to be a special volunteer to get into the PT Boat service, they said. You had to be an unusual physical specimen, they said. You had to be a highly trained specialist and all-round man for this rough and dangerous service, they said. Men of steel, boats of wood, and that sort of thing.

That was what I thought before some guy on the dock at Pearl Harbor told the guy in the signal tower to stop a passing PT Boat and put me on board. Nobody ever asked me if I wanted to be a PT sailor.

I spent the entire war trying to figure out how I managed to qualify. I was 6'2" and weighed 125 pounds with my shoes on. I had six weeks of boot camp and about four weeks of radar school—not enough to make me exactly overtrained.

As a kid I got a queasy stomach on a swing set. I could get carsick on a twenty-mile auto trip and almost get a stomach upset looking at water swish in the bathtub. Therefore the Navy chose to put me on the one vessel that most likely would make me seasick. They really should have given me a chance to volunteer before consigning me to a big surfboard that smashed and crashed over and through waves, putting you up to your neck in seawater.

A sailing trip on the three-masted barque *Elissa* out of Galveston last year, with a seasick potion behind my ear and another in my stomach, reminded me how miserable the world looked when we were going over one wave and through the next one.

Since I was a radarman, I got to look at a little scope with a sweep that went around and around while the boat climbed and dropped and vibrated. A vessel that travels at close to fifty miles an hour jumps from one wave to another or plows into it like a brick wall. The sensation was not the gentle sinking feeling you have with the roll of a large ship. It was one of falling until the boat hit bottom, then the deck would come flying at you and whop you if you didn't allow some spring in your legs to absorb the shock.

To see the radar, I had to cover my head with a canvas hood.

This narrowed my little world to the inside of a box that was being kicked down several flights of stairs. The shock of the hull hitting the trough of the sea would knock the sweep clear off the radar scope. And the radioman, Cusack, sat across from me in the tiny charthouse smoking a cigar. Take all this, and you have created the sickest, most miserable PT sailor in history.

We clung to the gun to keep from being washed overboard because in a rough sea we were sometimes up to our necks in water. I felt fortunate we weren't sent to the Aleutian Islands, where PT crew stood ice-floe watches from the bow. If they were forgotten for five or ten minutes, someone had to use ice picks to break the ice coating off them.

I never got seasick at the helm because it was a constant fight to keep the boat on course and from digging too deeply into a wave. Unfortunately, the executive officer had a weak stomach, too, and he reserved the wheel watch for himself. So when there was nothing else to do, I clung to a torpedo, swallowing salt water as it washed over me and returning it periodically. There may be a worse feeling than flopping on a wet deck like a mullet out of water, but I don't know what it is.

Once we were the flagship and were making a torpedo run in fleet maneuvers off Hawaii in stormy seas near the Molokai Channel. The skipper asked me for a bearing. Instead of addressing him, I addressed a bucket I had clasped between my knees. The torpedo run went to pot, and the squadron commander spent the rest of the night gathering up boats scattered all over the Hawaiian Islands. And this was a proud, battle-ready outfit. The crews had worked hard and were really very proficient.

The squadron didn't start out to be an eight-ball outfit. Its 78-foot Huckins boats were better built and could outmaneuver the Higgins and outrun the Elco PT Boats. But there were no spare Huckins parts in the South Pacific war zone. So we were the "4F Squadron." It's difficult to admit that you didn't serve on John Kennedy's boat, but to admit you served in Ron 26 is something else again.

Another squadron went south, four of the eight boats remained in Pearl Harbor, and we went west to Midway Island to commune with the gooney birds. And the rest of the crew deteriorated to my unseamanlike level. An outfit that gathers seashells and Japanese fishing balls is not exactly on combat duty. Our most interesting hobby was watching the progress the salt-water termites were making in a hole in the keel, a job they did not complete in those two years.

Although the war had moved on, Marine and Navy forces

were still required at that outpost in the middle of the Pacific. Patrol duty there was extremely boring. At all times one boat anchored on 24-hour patrol on the channel between Midway's Eastern and Sand islands. One would be on standby and the other two on call.

The duty boat was always ready to get under way immediately to rescue survivors from downed aircraft. Planes were stored in the open, among the sand dunes. Crashes were not uncommon, and the squadron, serving as crash boats, rescued a number of downed pilots.

Routine tied to the buoy was hours and hours of card games, fishing, and swimming. We were in constant contact with the island through blinker signals from a tall tower. Sometimes we had to wake the radioman to decode messages.

Then one night the signal tower departed from procedure, announcing in a loud voice over the radio that a Japanese submarine had been spotted offshore and giving a specific location not far from our anchorage. We were quickly under way, quartermaster plotting the course, torpedomen setting depth-charge depths. Then we fired our first shot. The explosion was tremendous. The motor mechs down below said they were knocked about by the force of the charge.

Immediately the radio came alive. "Belay that! Belay that! Don't drop any more charges. Repeat. DO NOT drop depth charges."

It seemed strange that we were pulled out of the attack before it got started good. Later someone explained why. Midway is a giant coral reef that grew like a huge pancake on top of an extinct volcano. The fear was that an underwater explosion could dislodge the reef and possibly sink the whole island, something persistent bombing by the Japanese was unable to do during the pivotal 1942 battle.

That sort of took the satisfaction out of firing a shot in anger.

(November 13, 1985/December 31, 1974/December 10, 2009)

The greatest danger
the 259 boat ever faced
was from the U.S. Navy.

Ex-PT sailors are having another bull session, but I won't go because I never have any good war stories to tell. I can't compete with guys who survived two or three sinkings, with all sorts of kill notches on their torpedo tubes.

The greatest danger the 259 boat ever faced was from the United States Navy. They didn't exactly shoot at us. They just made us an experimental boat, which was almost as dangerous as being shot at. Maybe they didn't want to waste any of their combat boats with such missions.

These ideas were hatched by the base force, which hadn't swallowed a whole lot of salt water.

The first was to mount a set of twin .30-caliber machine guns outside the forward hatch. This was the hatch over the crew's quarters in the bow. This portion of the boat was frequently under water. At my battle station was a 20-millimeter cannon. A few feet back of that was a spot frequently waist deep in water. We held on to our cannon to keep from washing overboard.

They chose a nice day for the experiment, but by the time we were out to sea, we were in heavy swells. With skill at the helm, the bow could be held up for a time but not all the time. The machine guns were set up, and the gunner stood on the ladder, where the footing wasn't very good in a calm sea.

The first wave washed the gunner into the galley. Several hundred gallons of seawater soaked our bunks and lockers. A couple of more waves filled the bilges. More water came in before the gun could be secured and the hatch closed. We spent weeks cleaning and fighting mildew and cussing idea men.

A short time later someone got the bright idea of trying out a 90-millimeter Army mortar. It would be just the weapon for lobbing shells into Japanese troop barges, they said. They (whoever they were) had never been on a boat with a rounded bottom and moving slow. Sights aimed level could be pointing at the water before the weapon fired.

The mortar was designed to sit on solid earth. Not only could it not come anywhere close to the target, but it played havoc with the plywood deck, which wasn't designed to catch cavorting elephants. Recoil from the mortar caused work for the base carpenters.

The next idea was a water-oil fueled smokescreen generator. This, too, was a piece of Army equipment. It was supposed to cause enough smoke to hide half the Pacific Ocean. It started out well enough, spitting out a thick cloud of smoke. Then the thing blew its top, and the deck was covered with flames very near the vents to our gasoline tanks, which carried 300 gallons of 100 octane.

I grabbed a CO^2 fire extinguisher and the wind blew all the fog away. I hadn't touched the flames, but I did freeze my hand to the horn of the extinguisher. Cooler heads bailed buckets of water from the sea and washed the burning oil overboard.

We looked around and our Army instructor was on the bow, wearing a life vest and with his hand in the ring, ready to abandon ship. If the gasoline, four torpedoes, eight depth charges, and assorted ammunition had gone, he would have had a head start.

Next they needed a craft fast enough to drop depth charges and be clear in case they went off too soon. The 259 was fast. A slower vessel would have lost its fantail in the shallow explosion.

During the war we were never in any real danger, except, that is, from the U.S. Navy. That isn't a very good war story.

(May 12, 1983)

An *Old Man and the Sea* plot . . .

If you've already heard this story, don't stop me. It has an *Old Man and the Sea* plot as the PT 259 alternated between its stations in the boat harbor and the buoy at the entrance to the channel leading into the Midway Island lagoon. Twenty-four hour crash boat duty at the buoy was extremely boring. We cleaned our already spotless guns, played cards, and stared off over the reef to a horizon we never really saw any more.

One afternoon someone threw a cigarette overboard and the water whipped. Fish there struck anything white or shiny. We got out hooks and started fishing with droplines. Soon we had a bushel of Hawaiian bonita. We gave them to the base force guys who motored out in a launch to bring us supper. Schools of bonita went out to sea at the same time every afternoon. The base force was happy with our offerings. One day the chow was particularly bad, and we decided to cook some of our fish. They were delicious, a cross between tuna and chicken.

This sparked our interest in fishing. Our efforts drew the interest of a huge fish down on the bottom. We rigged a big hook with meat, tied it to a heavy cord, and dropped it overboard. We had a perfect view of the action. Even at six fathoms, the water was crystal clear. We could see all the corroded 50-caliber ammunition the air service stuck us with so they wouldn't have to clean it. It "accidentally" fell overboard while we were wrestling with it.

There was other jettisoned debris already covered by barnacles and coral. From a dark area near the channel edge, the big fish appeared. He circled the bait three or four times. Then he swam out about ten yards and stopped. Suddenly he was a streak headed for the bait, hit it, and didn't even tremble. The line broke. We got bigger line and a bigger hook. Again the line snapped. Then came a bigger line and a huge hook. The line held, but the monster straightened the hook out.

A base force machinist made an even bigger hook. Our fish, which we learned was a king-sized alaluwa, a Hawaiian delicacy, seemed to be enjoying the fame.

We were at the buoy one day in four. On the off-days we talked and schemed about how we were going to hook the rascal. We looked forward to going back to the buoy.

Our machinist finally prepared the ultimate in hooks. It was steel, as big as your hand. Our friend took a good look at the bait. He circled half a dozen times. Then he drew back farther than usual and made a magnificent lunge. Twenty-seven tons of boat shuddered. The line twanged—and went slack. The line, tied to a stanchion, had no give to it. The hook straightened again. If we had had a fishing rig, we would have fought him and worn him down. We didn't, so we ordered a super hook of tempered steel from the machine shop. We kept looking at our friend, waiting for our weapon to be forged.

Early one morning the fishing boat from the island passed. A guy with a deep ocean rig hooked our fish. The boat turned back to the lagoon, where the professional fisherman fought the monster for hours before he boated it. They took it back to base as a trophy and probably officers' mess.

Our hook was ready but we had no fish. We moped and time hung heavy again. We talked about sinking that fishing boat. Instead, the fisherman caught a tiger shark, so big it wouldn't fit on the scales, not fifty yards from the buoy where we swam. We figured we were even. We lost interest in fishing and swimming and took up poker again.

(October 26, 1983)

The rescuer was Hagerty.

After a few months on the island, the war was no longer real. And it seemed to matter little if it ended, for we were convinced no one of importance knew we were there.

But we had our own little wars. Once the crew of the Nine Boat ambushed the Six Boat at daylight when they came to relieve us at the buoy. We had a supply of eggs that had been in cold storage too long.

As the Six Boat cut its Packard marine engines to a bubbling idle and the crew was sleepily standing by to catch the "monkey paw" from the throw line to transfer the anchor line, we let 'em have it with two dozen eggs. Someone actually gave the executive officer scrambled egg on his ensign's cap. And eggs smashed over the decks, cockpit, and gun mounts.

The Six Boat came alive. Her three engines roared, and she was off in a cloud of spray. She stopped out in the middle of the lagoon. We wondered if they were reporting us to the commanding officer.

They weren't. They came at us in a wide-open attack at forty-five knots. The boat came right at us and cut a sharp starboard turn. All ten crewmen let go barrages of eggs. Our second barrage smashed against the hull and side of the Six Boat as she raised in the turn and her wake nearly turned us over. Eggs smashed all over everything. Each guy must have thrown four eggs. That ended the battle. But it gave us something to do for the next week. Scrub the boat and then repaint everything.

The next war happened on our own boat in forward crew's quarters between Hagerty and Little Willie. They never liked each other, Hagerty, the Bostonian, and Willie, the Kentucky coal miner's son. They had never gotten to finish the fight they started at the party back at Hilo. We had been waiting for months for it to resume.

It did during a marathon poker game. Willie had a full house. "What you got?"

"Just two little pairs," Hagerty gloated, "of jacks."

He reached for the pot.

"Just a minute," Willie said. "You have four of a kind. But you called 'em two pairs. That's what you have—two pairs." He reached for the money.

"The hand speaks for itself," Hagerty said, not letting the money go. They stood up.

War was at hand. It didn't last long. Willie shoved Hagerty so he could get at him. But Hagerty slid across the boat and crashed into a mahogany closet door, splitting it in half.

That ended the war. Willie and Hagerty became quick allies in repairing the door before the skipper came back aboard. The Yankee motor mechanic and the Rebel torpedoman made a great team. They took the door off its hinges and glued and clamped it. If you looked real close, you could see a fine line in the middle of the door. The skipper never noticed it.

Then we didn't have much to look forward to. Willie and Hagerty not only never fought again, they even started talking to each other. And then there was the time Hagerty came to the rescue.

This had happened at Pearl Harbor. Our base was the old Pearl City Yacht Club, a beautiful place with sloping lawns and coconut palms, with PT Boats clustered along a pier. They were eight or ten deep, which meant you had to jump from boat to boat to reach yours. The main problem was getting back to your boat in complete darkness. There were boats from three different squadrons of three different types—Elcos, Higgins, and Huckins.

Each type had a different superstructure with ammunition boxes and radar towers and other obstructions in different alignment. I knew where all our gun mounts and depth charge racks were, but I could never remember how those other boats were arranged. Even when you knew what boats were where, you could count on skinning your shins at least twice a trip.

This blind obstacle course was considerably more hazardous after a trip to Pearl City Tavern. Drunken sailors crashed through hatches, bounced off torpedoes, kicked depth charges, and generally destroyed themselves trying to get back to their own bunks.

Hagerty and Radioman Cusack made it back from Pearl City before curfew, but they sat down inside the gate to continue their barroom conversation. They were feeling no pain. Alcohol brewed from sugar cane and aged three weeks had that effect. But the anesthetic definitely wore off by morning when it settled in the eyeballs and exploded.

The nightly poker game was under way by the time Cusack and Hagerty set out down the pier looking for the Nine Boat. I couldn't blame them for choosing the wrong cluster in the dark. That meant a lot of extra bruises. Even sober guys had made that mistake. This night we were the outboard boat. We could hear bumps, crashes, and lots of cussing as Cusack and Haggerty stumbled and fell through the dark. Then there were a couple of thumps on our deck, some heavy walking, and Cusack shouted, "Man overboard!"

Everyone dived overboard looking for poor old Hagerty. We had some strong swimmers. They dived and dived into the oily gunk the Japanese had so badly polluted the year before.

It was no use. Hagerty was gone.

"Whas goin' on?" a voice asked from the deck above.

"Hagerty fell overboard," someone yelled back.

"Thass terrible," he said, ripping off his jumper and jumping into the water. The rescuer was Hagerty. He had managed to swim under the boat and had climbed up on the other side.

Somehow it made us feel better that Hagerty was willing to risk his life for a shipmate, even if it was himself.

(April 7, 1981/June 25, 1986)

Boris Karloff proved to be a genius of an actor . . .

Walter Stoops was a Marine pilot with VMR 953, flying twin-engine C-46 transport planes out of Ewa Naval Air Station near Pearl Harbor to Bougainville, Guadalcanal, the Philippines, China, and later Japan, but he took one of his most memorable flights as a copilot on a trip between French Frigate Shoals and Midway Island to rescue Boris Karloff and the other members of his "Arsenic and Old Lace" performing group.

"One of our planes taking the troupe to Midway Island had engine trouble and had to set down on French Frigate Shoals. We took an empty plane out, picked them up, and took them on to Midway," Stoops said.

"The troupe was overjoyed to see us. They were really glad to get off that rock."

I can understand the actors' feelings. But their joy at leaving likely was only a fraction of the joy the occupants of that godforsaken place felt at seeing them. I can only imagine the happiness of the men at French Frigate Shoals at having the company of real female women right there on their little chunk of real estate.

Their domain was a reef 600 miles or so northwest of Honolulu, where Seabees landed bulldozers, scooped up coral, and bulkheaded it, creating a rectangular island the shape of a flight deck. There were two Quonset huts and a contingent of the most rock-happy sailors you ever saw.

This was an emergency landing field and a fueling stop. There was absolutely nothing on the rock for men to do but look for seashells, watch the same movies over and over until they were replaced, and read and re-read whatever books and magazines were there.

The visit of a theatrical troupe that brought feminine voices and the smell of perfume was probably one of the high points in the lives of the poor jokers who were stationed there for three years—duty worse than a penitentiary sentence.

"'That was a short runway. You made a pass over it before you landed. Then you put the wheels down inches from the edge so you would stop in time. With the other plane parked on the strip, there was really barely enough room to land," Stoops said.

He was flying as co-pilot and had time to visit with the passengers. Members of the troupe signed Stoops' Short Snorter $1 U.S. dollar bill with "Hawaii" printed on it. Regular bills were unacceptable. The bills were marked to prevent use of money captured by the Japanese when they overran Pacific islands.

Short Snorters were an informal group of pilots and crewmen who qualified by flying across an ocean. They collected paper money in various countries and pasted them together like modern folds of credit cards. Stoops has about fifty of these bills.

Signing his bill as nearly as he could determine were Karloff, Walter Plimpton, James Haynes, Dave Carson, Tom Roch, Pat Lolvinel, Sam Ferrig, Jean Burlye, L. Cary, Maziel Elebrie, Sleepy Kennedy, Gilbert Meston, and P. C. Skeinley. It was dated 4-16-44.

"Boris Karloff was one of the most gracious persons I have ever met," Stoops said.

Tonight Vincent Price will present a tribute to Karloff at the Academy of Motion Picture Arts and Sciences as part of an event marking the 100th anniversary of Karloff's birth. Price said the actor, who died in 1969, wanted to be remembered as a serious actor and chafed under the Hollywood stereotyping that stifled his considerable talents and preferred him in roles like that of his famous portrayal of Frankenstein.

I have no trouble at all remembering Boris Karloff as a genius of an actor, who proved it under the most adverse of conditions, the 1944 visit to the Pacific that Stoops described and the Midway presentation of "Arsenic and Old Lace."

First I was impressed with him as a person. The women in the cast went immediately to the officers' club, where they were the center of attention. I was always impressed with how the Navy looked after the men so that looking at real, live American women would not make them think impure thoughts. In officers' country there were no concerns that the gentlemen there would have any untoward images in their heads, even though there were no other women within a thousand miles—not even natives.

Karloff came to the enlisted men's chow hall and waited in line with the rest of us. He could have done much better at the officers' mess, because the food was much better there. I know this because our boat had a baker working in their kitchen, and he kept us well supplied with steaks and other goodies from officers' stores—much better stuff than Spam and Australian mutton in the enlisted kitchen.

While he ate, the actor was very dignified. He told anecdotes as we crowded around. He also was sympathetic and asked questions about life on a sand spit in the backwashes of the war. He carried on an entertaining conversation for a couple of hours.

Later the troupe put on several performances at the island theater. The audience was composed of guys eighteen to twenty-five years old who had been on the island for a year or more. Midway was an air and submarine base, and not much was going on there except poker games. The inhabitants had what was called the "Midway stare."

Only a newcomer noticed it. Within several months he too was staring at the horizon. When a guy was talking to someone, his eyes still focused on the horizon, seemingly looking right through the person he was addressing.

It was almost impossible to enjoy a movie, because the sailors and Marines were so affected by the sight of females on the screen—no matter what the age—that they yelled, whistled, and stomped on the floor, making it difficult to hear any dialogue.

I fully expected that sort of behavior at the play. The women were dressed and made up as little old ladies, but the guys knew they were actually good-looking chicks under that makeup.

And the men were rowdy when the play opened. There were whistles and some wise remarks. But they soon died down as the audience began to follow the story, captivated by the performance of Boris Karloff.

They were no longer aware that there were females on the stage. Karloff was magnificent. He was in complete control. The theater was quiet except for bursts of laughter that lines of the play produced. These were young men who were starved for female companionship. In the middle of the broad Pacific, this was as close as they were going to get to American womanhood.

Yet Boris Karloff, with his great performance, made them forget all those painful yearnings and concentrate on the play. A serious dramatic actor? That's the way I remember him.

He was the champ!

(January 18/January 22, 1988)

There was one thing
I never did learn.

A TV commercial about how much a young person can learn in the service set me to thinking what I learned in the U.S. Navy.

I learned how to get out of a skin-tight jumper at 3 a.m. without choking to death. I learned never to do anything I wasn't told to do because they'd remember me for the next work detail. I learned never to half-smile when an officer was talking because he could interpret that as silent insubordination.

But there was one thing I never did learn. That was semaphore, the wigwag language spoken by waving two sticks with flags on them to spell out messages between ships. I learned all the alphabet, holding the flags like they told me to for each letter.

But when someone was sending me a message, it was mirror backwards. I could send messages, but I couldn't receive at all.

There was always someone around who could read the stuff, I said. But one time nobody else was around. That's when I got in trouble.

Our PT Boat escorted a couple of sampans of Marines out to Kure Island for maneuvers. Kure is way out next to nothing except the International Date Line. It is occupied by sea lions, seals, and a gaggle of gooney birds, frigate birds, boobies, and terns.

I paddled a little walnut shell of a dinghy more than a mile to shore to deliver a message. I looked back to see people on the boat jumping up and down and waving. I waved back. Mitch, a motor mech, got out the flags.

He waved a quick message. Then a slow message. I still couldn't read it. I turned my back to them and looked over my shoulder. By then I was too confused to read anything. Cusack the radioman tried the blinker signal light. That was worse.

I could tell the message was urgent, so I paddled furiously across the lagoon. Half a mile away I could hear them shouting. One was still trying to signal with the flags.

I paddled closer. Then I got the message. "Get the beer from the Marines."

There was only a small ration, and if it wasn't picked up soon, the Marines would surely quaff it all down.

I paddled back to the beach in record time. Only half the ration was left. I was so unpopular when I got back, I donated my share to the pot. That was nice, because they had already voted and I didn't have a share.

To make up for the shortage, they drank what was left as fast as they could. They were happy with the effect. Quartermaster Petroski drained his last bottle and threw it out the porthole. It didn't go out. It cracked the glass, which was battened closed.

That would be a hard one to explain. Luckily the officers were ashore sharing libation with Marine officers.

We left the port open so it wouldn't be visible. It didn't work. Mr. Reid, the skipper, saw it right away and demanded to know how the window got cracked.

"I think it was a ricocheting bullet, sir," Hagerty said right away.

The Marines had been plinking away at bottles, Japanese fishing balls, and frigate birds with their carbines.

Mr. Reid had Cusack contact the Marine commander with a stern protest. I can only imagine that the rest of the exercise by the Marine group was strictly business. I imagine some jarheads got chewed out royally.

I didn't feel much sympathy for them. They deserved as much for drinking up beer rightfully belonging to the U.S. Navy.

I spent the rest of that cruise practicing semaphore. I was glad nobody ever called on me to use it again.

(November 21, 1980)

We listened to stories about depth charge attacks . . .

The visit of the USS *City of Corpus Christi* takes me back to when I was a little kid and two World War I submarines called on the Port of Corpus Christi. The subs had numbers but not names. They seemed big to me because I was so little. I remember waiting for my Aunt Pearl to come down the ladder. She was about five feet tall and about that wide, and I was afraid she might get stuck in the hatch. Apparently the sailors were, too, for they jumped to help her.

Compared to the World War II models, those subs were tiny. Living conditions were primitive, and the ventilating system wouldn't give one much encouragement to leave the surface.

World War II submarines were a vast improvement, but the crews slept on top of torpedoes. Space between some bunks was so narrow a sailor had to get out of bed to turn over. Most other sailors wanted no part of submarine service and its cramped life way under the water. I could sympathize with that view. Sometimes it was days before crewmen got a look at the outside world.

But when I was on the Nine Boat, bouncing around on the surface, I thought of submarines. As I flopped about on the deck, alternately retching and holding my breath under water as waves rolled me and I held on to keep from washing overboard, I thought about those poor guys cooped up down there, gliding along silently in air-conditioning and even in dry bunks. No rolling and pitching.

Then I got acquainted with some of the pigboat occupants on Midway Island. They were always disgusted to find they had returned from a war patrol to a remote sand spit instead of the Royal Hawaiian Hotel back at Honolulu, a submarine recreation palace.

We listened to stories about depth-charge attacks and how many of the "bloopers" nearly got them. Some of the conning towers were nearly covered with painted ships representing the tonnage the subs had sunk.

One boat limped in with the conning tower caved in. It looked like a child had been beating on a beer can with a ball-peen hammer. The periscope stuck off to one side at right angles. The planking on the deck was splintered. It had survived repeated depth-charge attacks. Seams were split and electrical equipment was damaged. One more depth charge could have finished her off.

After talking to members of the crew and seeing the results of a prolonged attack on a vessel lying helpless on the bottom, I decided the bouncing salt water topside wasn't so bad after all.

(March 16, 1983)

I never met Mr. Fitzgerald's boy.

I was always sorry I didn't look up the Fitzgeralds' son. They lived next door to my mother in Kingsville, Texas. They had moved there from Bishop, where Mr. Fitz had been manager of the farm implement store. They were good neighbors, always doing things for Mamma. They were extremely proud of their sons, Ralph and Carl. They were both good students and then they were in the service. Ralph was off taking pilot training when I went into the Navy.

"Ralph's in the Pacific," Mr. Fitz said. "Maybe you'll run across him out there."

I said I'd keep an eye out for him. But I never expected to see him. For one thing, I was not going to be an officer. And he was already a commissioned pilot. Even that early I had a suspicion I wouldn't be hanging out much in officers' country. I went through my training, attended service school, and was soon fighting the war of boredom in the Central Pacific. Sometimes we went on maneuvers. A few times we were on alert. Occasionally we performed crash-boat duty—searching for and rescuing downed pilots.

But mostly we sat. We scraped our boat and painted it. We broke down our guns, cleaned, and oiled them. We took the torpedoes apart and put them together. We played poker until it got so boring we played Old Maid, cribbage, pinochle, and other games I've forgotten. A number of times we rushed to crash scenes. Rarely did we rescue a pilot. Occasionally we recovered bodies. And our boats took island dead far out to sea for burial ceremonies.

I had written home about the antics of the gooney birds without naming them. I was trying to let Mamma know I was out at Midway Island. Mr. Fitz read the letter and told her where I was. He had been in the Navy in World War I and was familiar with the Laysan albatross.

I was in the same part of the world as Ralph, he told my mother. If I inquired around, there was a good chance we could get together, Mr. Fitz said. I really didn't do much inquiring around. We seldom had much to do with the airedales. Sometimes they came along for a ride with us. But not many of us accepted their offer to ride with them. Their planes sat out among the dunes. Their engines seemed to fail at very inopportune times. We didn't aspire to take our last voyage in a canvas sack.

So I never met Mr. Fitzgerald's boy. He had been an honor student at the University of Texas. He was looking forward to a career in law, I think.

The days droned on. We alternated. One day on standby, one day at the buoy at the channel entrance, and two days off to work on the boats. We were on buoy duty when one of the guys on deck saw the crash.

"A SBD went straight in," he yelled. "It didn't pull out."

The crash was on the far side of the lagoon. We raced around the island and could see the wreckage among the reefs. But we couldn't get through the coral reefs and pinnacles. A longboat from the island reached the scene. By the time we came back in, the longboat had retrieved the bodies. They were under a canvas tarp on the dock.

"The pilot was a Lt. Fitzgerald," someone said.

Later I found out he was from Kingsville, Texas. I felt terrible. I knew how crushed the Fitzgeralds would be. All their hopes for their son died when he was killed on a crummy island in a crummy plane that wouldn't fly right.

I had to tell Mr. Fitz what happened. It was wrong that I didn't try to look him up. That would have meant something to the Fitzgeralds. I still feel guilty about that, forty years later. Especially on Memorial Day.

(May 28, 1984)

The ensign did not like onions.

Come January 1 a lot of Navy officers are going to have to make some New Year's resolutions. They'll have to resolve to make their beds. The new order says those from lieutenant commander downward will make their own bunks and tidy up their quarters without help from Navy stewards. It doesn't apply to the guys with scrambled eggs on their hats. The guys who wear white hats are not likely to break into tears at this news.

But the Navy announcement made me think of my old white hat and an unnamed ensign from Iowa. The ensign and I didn't hit it off right from the start, all because he didn't know that the mode of expression on that tiny bit of the Pacific Ocean happened to be sarcasm. On his first day aboard our little craft, I had taken the radar transmitter apart for cleaning. Bits and pieces of the gear were scattered about the deck.

"Whatcha doing?" asked this pudgy guy with the untarnished gold braid. He was to be our only officer for weeks at a time.

My answer would have been acceptable to any island-happy slob who had been on that rock for two years. I said, "I'm planting watermelon seeds. What the —do you think I'm doing?"

Unfortunately, the ensign had not been out there for two years. He was part of a replacement contingent sent out to "square away" what the brass called an "unmilitary situation" among the men. I became his personal project. Therefore all crud details were mine. One was to "clean up my stateroom and make up my sack."

The staterooms on a PT Boat were so tiny they didn't take much cleaning. I cleaned the deck, bulkheads, and overhead. I even dusted the desk, though there wasn't a fleck of dust in a thousand miles. Deliberately, I did not make his bed.

"Hey," he said peevishly. "You didn't make up my sack!"

"No, sir. That's because I am not a steward's mate, sir."

A wise old sea lawyer had told me only stewards were required to make officers' beds, according to the gospel of Navy Regulations. The ensign was enraged. He poured it on everyone now. He started telling the rates how to do their jobs.

Soon they were doing only what he ordered, and the boat was

falling apart. And the ensign refused to take part in the normal routine of life, such as a turn at cooking.

The crew discussed the problem. Then the silent treatment started. No conversation. Poker games folded when he sat down. But the ensign proved tough. He kept to his stateroom and ignored the crew.

Then a torpedoman made a fine discovery. The ensign did not like onions. Not only did he not like onions, he would gag on anything that had so much as a trace of onion cooked into it. When we loaded stores, we took on a big new supply of onions. Soon the galley smelled like a hamburger den. Oatmeal, eggs, potatoes, meat, everything had onion cooked into it. Two meals did the job. After the dinner dishes were put away, the young executive officer came to the forward crew's quarters with this painful announcement:

"Tell you what, fellows. I don't think I fully understood the situation out here. In the future if you treat me right, I promise I'll treat you right."

That was fair enough, and he would later prove it by scraping and sanding his square of boat bottom when we hit drydock.

"How would you like your steak cooked, sir?" a gunner's mate asked.

"Without onion," he grinned.

The ensign was squared away. The military establishment had lost another one.

(December 11, 1974)

Pineapple juice—
a perfectly nice,
pure, healthful drink

"Delicious," I said. "What is it?"

She mumbled something that sounded like ham.

"Not ham," I said, "but it's good whatever."

"I didn't say HAM. I said SPAM."

"Oh," I said, turning it over with a fork to see if there were any bugs in it. I tasted it again. Spam. A long time ago I swore a vile oath I would never, never, if I lived to be 120, take another bite of Spam.

I looked at it again. "Hamburger was $2.09 a pound," she said.

"You know," I said, "that Spam ain't half bad."

Maybe the difference was in the Navy cooking. You have a tendency to forget what a Navy cook sauced on vanilla extract could do to a pot of beans. Or even when he had sworn off the extract or Aqua Velva. It's not easy to have beans burned on the outside and raw in the middle. You get prejudiced against some things after being uncommonly familiar with them for months and months.

Take pineapple juice. It's a perfectly nice, pure, healthful drink. But there we were in the Hawaiian Islands where we were served pineapple juice three times a day, pineapple ice cream, pineapple pie, pineapple salad, pineapple, and Spam. The Navy was Dole's best customer. And sometimes we'd tie up our boat alongside a pineapple barge and we'd whack open fresh pineapples and munch the fresh pulp.

It was some time later when my prejudice against it developed, after we moved away from all that fresh greenery. The pipeline from the Dole plant continued, and I went to the galley for a cup of pineapple juice six or eight times a day.

The days grew into weeks and months and to a year or more. There was little entertainment, and the nearest female companionship was more than a thousand miles away.

It was about this time I developed symptoms that suggested that female companionship of a very low and infectious order had been much closer. This could not be remotely possible, I told myself.

I worried and I brooded. How could it be? I remembered all the various movies the Navy had shown us on what terrible things can happen to you if you get too friendly with the opposite sex. They also showed us pictures of sailors torn apart by automobiles, and when they finally let us out of boot camp into San Diego, we were afraid to cross a street or talk to girls. All those training films said bathroom fixtures didn't transmit this type of ailment, and that's the only place I had been.

Finally I could stand it no longer. In the very strictest of confidence, I told a shipmate of my embarrassing problem. He didn't take the confidence lightly. He jumped on it with both feet. He hooted and doubled up laughing. The rest of the crew assembled to see what was so godawful funny on that godforsaken rock. With tears streaming down his face, he announced that I thought I had a social disease in the middle of the Pacific Ocean, where no woman had set foot for years. It was probably a good thing. Crew members had been fighting and snarling at each other. They needed a good laugh. Only they laughed for a week.

Actually I wasn't very embarrassed. I was too relieved to find the horrible symptom could be cured by drinking a quart of water. But I'm still afraid to drink pineapple juice—just in case.

(May 14, 1979)

The crew was surprised to see Hansard and Hall talking.

Hansard and Hall didn't like each other at all. They had nothing in common. Hall grinned a lot with a buck-toothed smile. He was a Hoosier and something of a talker. Hansard seldom talked. Yet he was irritating. It wasn't anything he did. His teeth always needed brushing, and he was unkempt. His curt way of speaking made him seem to be an arrogant slob. He had no friends.

They were bunkmates in the after crew's quarters. Sleeping was usually the only time they shared a room. That's why the crew of the 259 Boat was a little surprised to see them in an animated conversation. They weren't snarling or cussing each other. They were having a serious talk.

Both were model airplane nuts as kids. Now they found the blueprints for our PT Boat and decided to make an exact replica. They talked for two days about what they were going to need. They bought every ship and plane model from the island's Ship's Service Stor2e and wrote home for balsa wood, glue, and other supplies.

Pretty soon the motor mech and torpedoman avoided the rest of us. Hall dropped out of the continuous poker game and even quit listening to Jo Stafford records. Those were his only two interests, since there was nothing to drink and no women to chase. Now he and Hansard were always together, talking and planning.

When they got materials, they took over the charthouse, spreading out the blueprints and stacks of wood, glue, pins, knives, and razor blades. It was aggravating to squeeze through their boat works to get topside, but we didn't complain. The only other working area was the table in the forward crew's quarters, and that was reserved for poker.

When it was necessary to use the charthouse on Navy business, the two builders packed up all their supplies in a box and stowed it in a corner of the auxiliary engine room.

From the keel the ribs were carefully bent, and two layers of balsa wood perfectly imitated the double-planked mahogany hull of the PT. They crafted compartments and made furniture to scale. They spent days whittling out 20- and 40-millimeter machine-gun turrets. Torpedoes and depth charges were perfect miniatures.

They argued and conferred on each point. The charthouse was complete with tiny glass portholes. The radar mast was glued in position and imitation canvas glued over the decking. They machined out tiny rudders, shafts, struts, and propellers.

Months had passed since Hall and Hansard started the project. They wouldn't talk of anything else. Their model was painted with Navy gray and lacquered. It was a work of art, like the original in every detail. It was placed in the charthouse for all of us to see.

"Whatcha gonna do with it?" someone asked.

Both looked pained.

"First one stateside gets it," Hansard said.

"No way," Hall said. "You got six months on me."

The friendship was over. They snarled again. A fight was brewing. They finally threatened to smash up the little boat to settle the argument. Gus, the executive officer, overheard that.

"You can't do that," he said. He was one guy who really loved our boat, and he was being ordered home.

That's when we decided. Gus should have the model as a going-home present. It brought tears to his eyes. We didn't consult the builders, but they couldn't object. They never spoke to each other again, but they weren't fighting. And wherever Gus lives today, I'm betting the PT 259 dominates his mantelpiece.

(October 3, 1981)

It was strangely impressive to be marching in formation . . .

The sun beat down on us as we marched. It had been two years since most of us had marched at all, and our twelve-man crew had never marched as a unit. We had to have instructions on marching on the half step, pause, and half step of the funeral march. It was strangely impressive to be marching in formation, all the sailors and Marines on the island. I didn't know there were that many men on that sand spit.

The cadence of the funeral dirge seemed incredibly slow. The drumbeats echoed off the sand dunes. There was no talk, and the only spectators to the march were inattentive gooney birds. They could have cared less that their president was dead.

The news came as would a telegram announcing a death in the family. It was cruel, personal news that gave us an empty, lost feeling. He had been more than a president. He was like a golden voice from the clouds. So even now it isn't remarkable that Franklin Delano Roosevelt was born more than 100 years ago January 30. To those of us of that generation, he had lived forever. His was the voice of reason and hope in a nation that had lost hope. He was confident and reassuring.

I remember having to sit in a meeting of old people listening to Dr. Francis E. Townsend talk for old-age pensions. He was hostile to Roosevelt for not starting a pension. Roosevelt stole his thunder and started Social Security, and Townsend snorted that $60 a month was a miserable dole. Townsend was to be joined by Jewish-baiting fascists Gerald L. K. Smith and Father Charles E. Coughlin in opposition to Roosevelt before his movement crumbled.

There were others who complained about the government killing pigs and plowing under cotton to boost prices while people were ill clad and hungry. People joked about WPA workers leaning on shovels, but thousands of men were put to work and thousands of young men ate well and made a little money in the Civilian Conservation Corps.

I wasn't old enough to understand the NYA, NRA, PWA, and all the other programs that spawned the New Deal. I remember most people had the idea the president would fix what was wrong. As time went on, some people began calling him "That Man in the White House" to keep from using his name. They sort of snarled when they said it.

But Roosevelt had their number. He played to the radio audience like a symphony conductor. He destroyed his enemies with ridicule.

He couldn't be so commanding today. The television cameras would zoom in on his wheelchair and his polio-withered legs, and his image of iron strength would be destroyed. Photographers of Roosevelt's day would have considered that a cheap shot.

He had a way with words: "Nothing to fear but fear itself," "a day of infamy." Before he died, he wrote, "The only limit to our realization of tomorrow will be our doubts of today." He nearly led us through the war before he fell. Isolationists grumbled when he stoked the furnace of the great arsenal of democracy. Others accused him of being unprepared.

It didn't seem real there, standing on a Pacific runway. Sweltering sailors began to faint. We who were conditioned would make it. The commander gave a eulogy, and we were left to carry on without our leader. We didn't know a Harry S. Truman.

Nobody has felt comfortable with our last three presidents. That's a shame. I worried a lot less when I thought someone was at the helm of the ship of state.

(January 28, 1982)

We could smell a tropical rain, vegetation, flowers, the earth.

I swore if I ever got off that rock, I'd never give it a second thought. Then I opened this month's *National Geographic*, and I was right back in 1945. It has a pictorial study on the lesser Hawaiian Islands few people have heard of and very few have seen.

We were coming back from Midway Island to Pearl Harbor on small craft, and we got a good look along the way. We were already familiar with Kure Island out near the International Dateline. Kure is covered with seals and grouchy old sea lions who don't like their naps interrupted. We were wrestling with an old bull, and I grabbed his tail—a mistake. He flipped me about ten yards in the air.

And Pearl and Hermes Reef was a beachcomber's delight. We popped over the reef one dark night and spent days looking for an opening out. There was flotsam from the Pacific battles, Japanese fishing balls, and all sorts of wreckage.

The little islands were covered with sea turtles. Sharks were as thick as mullet in the water. We shot a few to feed the others and felt better paddling a paper-shelled dinghy ashore. I learned that when you turn over a 300-pound turtle, don't get your arm in the way. Their flippers are as hard as iron, and they have a punch like a mule.

We really didn't appreciate the voyage at the time. We just wanted to get home. You get that way after looking three years at the same ocean.

French Frigate Shoals had a landing strip and a small Navy contingent. The Seabees had built the landing strip on a coral reef, like a carrier deck in the middle of nowhere. I had seen "rock-happiness" on Midway. But those swabbies had vacant stares that went through you and the horizon and saw nothing.

Then a couple of Coast Guardsmen came through one of the world's highest surfs in a longboat to see us. Their station was a pinnacle thirty yards in diameter where they manned a weather station. We played softball, gave them our books and canned goods, and talked with those guys who swam among sharks as thick as minnows in a pool.

"Long as you got a tan, they won't bite," they said.

We lost a charthouse and were nearly toppled backward by combers sixty feet high as we sailed out through the surf. We got a good look at Niihau Island. There is a brilliantly white little beach around which cliffs rise hundreds of feet. There appeared to be a trail going up. A perfect island for exploring. But there was no bottom near the beach. No place to anchor, so we continued on at a slow pace to conserve fuel.

Then maybe 150 or more miles away from Niihau Island we smelled it. When the nose is removed from all contact with land atmosphere, it gets sharp. We could smell a tropical rain, vegetation, flowers, the earth. We could pick individual smells out of the air. Land. Not a sand spit. Real land. Hot damn!

Then there was Kauai, one of the most beautiful of the Hawaiian group, with the Sleeping Giant Mountain guarding the harbor. And there were people—civilians, kids, dogs, women. There was a real world out there after all.

The rest was receiving station, hurry up and wait, and finally the Golden Gate Bridge.

But out there past Kauai is a string of beauty now preserved as a wildlife refuge. I had a millionaire cruise right through the whole thing. But we really didn't see it in the going-home haze.

Someday I'd like to go back for a real look.

(May 18, 1978)

It was the slickest,
prettiest PT Boat
you ever saw.

Originally, Ron 26 was an efficient outfit. That changed after it was pulled out of a combat assignment to languish on Midway Island—a duty not designed to bring about military spit and polish. The uniform of the day became shorts and no shoes. We had suntan upon suntan and no military bearing at all.

"I'll put you on report," an ensign once threatened. "I'll restrict you to the boat."

"Whatever you say," the radioman answered. He never got off the boat anyway.

One Saturday Lt. Reid decided to throw an inspection. One day was pretty much like any other. The reason we knew it was Saturday was that he said he was holding a Saturday inspection. He came aboard wearing a crisp, ironed, khaki uniform. He saluted the ensign and the jack. That hadn't been done for a long time. He was followed by a yeoman with a clipboard to note violations.

When you think of a Navy inspection, you think of a formal one, sailors in dress uniforms, lined up on the deck of a battleship. This inspection was not formal. I was lying on my bunk when he came into the crew's quarters. He stood towering over me. Finally he said "Get up, Radar, I want to look under your sack."

That was the last inspection he pulled. Somehow it hadn't worked out according to the book.

The skipper did provide us with a form of recreation. He had been a relief pitcher for the Chicago White Sox, and he needed practice. The guys took turns playing catcher. Somebody found an old, worn-out catcher's mitt, padded with an old sock. I took a turn and he threw a fast ball. The padding slipped and my hand was blistered. It was sore for a week. That was the end of my Big League career.

To kill time we also gathered seashells and Japanese fishing balls, played cards, and for a while tied knots and made nets. We painted all handrails with white lead and wrapped them tightly with heavy cord. On each end we braided Turk's heads. It was nautical but not exactly Navy.

We covered the cord with varnish. In the charthouse there were stanchions and handrails over the ladder leading forward. These we painted black.

Somehow there wasn't enough thinner in the paint. It didn't dry. We really didn't know this until a new set of officers who had been sent to "straighten us out" came by in a real inspection—white gloves and all.

All three officers had black palms before they noticed. That was their last white glove inspection. After several months on the rock, the new officers were as nonchalant as their predecessors.

They didn't pay much attention to maintenance, but when it was time to paint the superstructure, they were around to supervise. The base was all out of regulation Navy gray paint. Through a joint effort, we attempted to duplicate it, using blue and white paint. It was a lot more blue than gray. Someone added a bunch of varnish.

It wasn't gray, but it was the slickest, prettiest dark blue you ever saw. PTs in jungle country were camouflaged green, but I never had seen one a shiny blue.

Neither had the brass at Pearl Harbor. The Nine Boat looked like a civilian yacht as the four boats churned up the channel past the fleet as we arrived back in Honolulu. An admiral on the bridge of an aircraft carrier was not amused. When we arrived at the PT base, there was an order waiting to return that boat to regulation color.

I had orders to come back to the States, so I was not involved. I suspect our officers were again on hand to oversee the repainting. A shame, too. It was the best paint job I ever saw in the Navy.

(September 16, 1982)

Tokyo Rose had Glenn Miller, Tommy Dorsey, the Andrews Sisters . . .

A few years ago people in this country might have been a bit upset if a president pardoned somebody accused of treason, as President Ford did his last day in office for the woman known as Tokyo Rose. Even back after the war it didn't seem to me that they ought to punish her for being a Pacific Theater disc jockey. For two years the only musical diversion a lot of us out there on remote Pacific "rocks" had was that sultry-voiced siren with a terrific collection of American records.

Our radio could pick up only two commercial-band stations. One was Tokyo. The other was Station WHO in Des Moines. The USA broadcast late at night was getting-up music for Midwest farmers. There were a lot of crop and market reports and hoedown music. But Tokyo Rose had Glenn Miller, Tommy Dorsey, the Andrews Sisters, and all the goodies they were playing back home. Of course, she did throw in a few little digs like, "How do you like it, boys, out there in those stinking jungles while your girlfriends are back home going out with those 4-F shipyard workers?"

That didn't worry me much because I didn't have a girl anyway. And they'd have American prisoners of war reading letters. It was bad propaganda because the men obviously had Japanese help in the writing. They were willing to talk so that their relatives back home would know they were alive. And besides, the music was great.

For that Iva Toguri D'Aquino was found guilty of treason and sentenced to ten years in prison. She served six.

That's why I dropped over to see my old friend and former colleague Kenneth McCaleb. He has a number of mementos picked up after he landed with the Army of Occupation as head of the Far East Bureau of International News Service. He picked up a wooden powder bowl and a teacup and saucer at her studio in the Radio-Tokyo Building.

"Actually, Tokyo Rose was more of a sidebar story at the time," McCaleb said. "So much was going on then. And a whole lot of the men had never heard of her. She gave a press conference later, and as I recall, the only question asked was if she was American. She said she was."

Reporters were busy covering the occupation and the displacement of the emperor by Gen. Douglas MacArthur. Then there were the war criminals. Ken and several other reporters located Hideki Tojo, Japanese prime minister when Pearl Harbor was attacked, in a Tokyo suburb. They had heard the Combat Intelligence Command was to arrest him.

CIC officers knocked on the door. Tojo appeared at a window. He was told he was under arrest. He asked, "Would you give me a moment to myself, please?"

He closed the shutters. A shot was heard. Reporters and soldiers rushed in to find Tojo lying over a love seat, shot under the heart. He regained consciousness and spoke. A Japanese translated for Ken. "I assume all responsibilities for the war. I thought it was a just war and for the good of the Japanese people and the people of East Asia. Now I know that war is not good for the people."

He said he chose the pistol for hara-kiri because he felt it more certain than the knife. "Please do not try to make me recover, Banzai!"

But the man who had been pictured over the world as one of the three great villains of all time—Hitler, Mussolini, and Tojo—did recover. American blood and medicine saved him so he could be tried and hanged as a war criminal December 23, 1948.

"I doubt there was really a Tojo as we knew him," Ken said. "In the Japanese view he was not a dictator."

But he and other architects of the war were tried and executed. And what about Tokyo Rose?

Ken shook his head. I seconded the motion. She was a victim of circumstances. Her main crime was being a bad DJ.

(*January 25, 1977*)

The serving lines were dishing out a turkey feast . . .

I got a note yesterday saying, "Tomorrow is the 40th anniversary of V-E Day. Can we do something?"

Well, okay, but I celebrate V-E Day on May 8.

On May 1, 1945, the Germans said Adolph Hitler was dead and Adm. Karl Doenitz was his successor. Berlin was captured by the Russians on May 2. On May 7 German Gen. Alfred Jodl signed the terms of unconditional surrender in the Allied headquarters in Reims, France. Lt. Gen. Walter B. Smith, Gen. Dwight Eisenhower's chief of staff, signed for the Allies.

The free world celebrated May 8 as Victory in Europe Day. On May 9 the surrender was ratified in Berlin, actually ending the war. So they ought to give us a three-day holiday.

But back on May 8, 1945, we were two days out of San Francisco aboard the Liberty Ship *George Clymer*, coming home. We were pleased because there was a saying in the Pacific, "Golden Gate in Forty-Eight. Bread line in Forty-Nine." We were ahead of schedule, and if things went right, the unpleasantness of all those rotten islands would be gone, and we wouldn't be back aboard another leaky tub heading the other way.

Words of announcements over the ship's loudspeaker rose and fell, fringed in static of the shortwave radio. Things were moving fast on the other side of the world, but there was little shouting on that ship. The Japanese weren't showing signs of giving up. To the guys in the Pacific, the European war was a long way off. Our enthusiasm was dimmed because we were out of the tropics. The weather was chilly and everyone had a bad cold.

The seas were rough and many of the soldiers on board were seasick. We didn't want to go below to our bunks because the smell there was enough to make you sick if the sea didn't. And the food didn't do much for the stomach, either. There was Australian mutton, as strong as a billy goat in heat, Spam, powdered eggs, and servings of greasy glop.

The chow line went by the officers' mess, where the ports were open and smells of finely prepared food wafted out. They ate real food. It stirred the digestive juices and got us in the mood to take on a real load of chow. But by the time we got to our chow hall, the smells changed. Some guys smelled it and threw up, causing others to put their trays back and walk out.

I had been sleeping on deck in the fresh air. But now it was too cold, and I had to go back to my bunk. This was when we received the news of the surrender in Europe. The groaning forms under the blankets could have cared less whether we won or lost.

That's when we got the surprise. The officers' mess smelled like they were having turkey and dressing. As the line progressed, we saw it was like Thanksgiving in there. Honest-to-goodness turkey in May. There was some grumbling about torturing the lowly enlisted men to the end. We'd have to go home to find a meal like that.

But, no, there it was. The serving lines were dishing out a turkey feast with gravy, mashed potatoes, cranberry sauce—the works. I still have that miraculous menu somewhere. We ate so much we almost made ourselves sick.

It only occurred to me later. Why were they saving all those turkeys? And what would they have done with them if V-E Day hadn't occurred? We only had a day more to reach port.

So you can go ahead and celebrate V-E-Day today, May 7. Me, I'm going to wait until tomorrow and have a turkey sandwich.

(May 7, 1985)

Kalmar taught me a lesson.

You meet a lot of guys in the service. Some of them are almost as close as kin. Then it's over and you never see each other again. I hadn't thought of Kalmar Snyder in half a century. He was a crewman on PT 260 and I was on PT 259. We really got acquainted when we returned to the States and embarked on some wild and woolly liberties in Boston. Sailors who haven't seen a woman or taken a drink in more than two years are inclined to live it up when they get back to civilization. When you are nineteen, you can take a lot of living it up.

A couple of times I had to practically carry him back to the base. We had a lot of long, rambling conversations and became pretty well acquainted. He was a fairly crude Indiana farm boy.

One night we were partying it up pretty good, laughing and telling jokes. It looked like the war was about over and we were in high spirits. Serveral of us were standing at the bar when an old man shuffled up and mumbled. Someone suggested that the bum ought to be thrown out. The old man was wrinkled and his eyes were red. Probably a wino. He mumbled some more and another sailor pushed him away.

"Wait a minute," Kalmar said. "Look at the calluses on this old fellow's hands. He was a working man and he's had a hard life. Let's buy him a drink."

The old man's hand shook. He looked us over and tears came to his eyes. He nodded and took the drink. The old man didn't really seem very interested in the drink. Later I wondered if he might have been an old sailor himself. Or maybe he had someone in the war.

Kalmar taught me a lesson. It doesn't hurt to be nice to someone, even if he might be a bum.

I hadn't thought of the incident until I attended a PT Boat reunion in Boston. There was a ceremony on the Battleship Massachusetts honoring shipmates who had died. The list was long. It included more than half of my crew—and Kalmar Snyder.

It was about this time of the year when Kalmar showed the kindness I remember him for. A small bit of Christmas spirit involving a fellow man. A toast to you, Kalmar.

(November 20, 2009)

Everyone can remember what he was doing on V-J Day.

Everyone can remember precisely what he was doing when he heard of some great event in history. That includes the bombing of Pearl Harbor, the death of President Roosevelt, V-E Day, the atom bombing of Japan, V-J Day, the assassination of President Kennedy, and others since.

The weakest recollection is of the B-29 bomber dropping a single bomb thirty-six years ago Thursday and incinerating Hiroshima and 100,000 of its residents. We who had never heard of atomic energy had a difficult time believing one bomb could do all that. The second bomb, on Nagasaki on August 8, 1945, was just as incomprehensible, but we saw it could end the war. That's the day I remember.

On August 15 we were lined up for inspection before going into Newport, R.I., on liberty. The loudspeaker announced the war was over. An officer waved us out. Civilian guards at the gate fired their pistols in the air—probably for the first time.

A big old boy from Indiana (I'll call him Ross) and I set out to celebrate. Ross was a little nuts but harmless. His buddies said his PT Boat caught a shell and exploded. He was the only crew member not killed or wounded. Both his skipper and executive officer were unconscious. Ross put the wounded, including his captain, in a life raft and pulled it away from the burning boat, swimming and grasping the tow line in his teeth. He swam back to the boat and set explosive charges to destroy the burning hulk. He swam to the raft and tended to the wounded until they were picked up. He did everything according to the book. Only they gave the skipper the Navy Cross. The other survivors got a unit citation. I could see that might make Ross unhappy.

The fellow in the liquor store was so happy at the war's end he sold us a bottle of prewar stuff at the regular price. We roamed the streets looking for something to do. I'd have a nip on the bottle. Ross would have two or three big gulps. The liquid fire almost paralyzed my throat. I sipped less and less, but Ross seemed to get thirstier as we walked along a seawall.

It was after midnight when a Marine came up from the beach. He had a problem. He and his buddy and some girls were having a blanket party down there on the sand. They had food, drinks, and one extra girl. They needed a date for her. The party was stalled. I said okay. Then I looked around and old Ross was sagging against a lamp post. His eyes were glassy. I started for the beach. After all, there were no girls in the Pacific, and we still might be going back.

I followed the Marine, then stopped. Ross was out of it. I couldn't leave him there. No telling the trouble he'd get into. The Marine set off to find someone else. He probably didn't have any trouble.

But I did. Ross wanted to take a punch at everybody on the bus back to the base. I had to hold him to keep us both from getting punched out by a mob. He was becoming a wild man. On base he screamed obscenities and dumped trash cans, tore down signs, including that of the officer of the day, and ripped up a picket fence before I could push him into the barracks.

We could have both landed in the brig. For years I've thought about that blanket party. It's my fantasy. I should have left Ross on the beach. But you don't do that to a hero.

Remember V-J Day? I'll never forget it.

(August 4, 1981)

The memory of a golden youth comes back . . .

Memorial Day 1985—This is the day when we are directed to lend our thoughts to those who died before their time in some war. I think of several guys I went to school with who didn't come back from World War II. Others died in Korea and some I knew less well in Vietnam. The passage of time seems to put them all in the same vague, all-but-forgotten vault where their memory seldom disturbs our everyday consciousness. The victims of all the wars sort of blend together, and as their survivors die off, they are remembered only on bits of eroding stone.

But I remember one fellow in particular. He was a perfect prototype of today's surfer—hair so blond you could think it was bleached. The whiteness of his hair contrasted sharply with the blueness of his eyes. He had a slender build and always seemed to be deeply tanned. He was "laid back" and "cool" many years before the terms were invented. His name was Robertson. All I knew was that he was from California. He had an easy, natural way of talking, full of confidence. He would have been a natural salesman.

We were both instructors at the Fleet Radar School at Camp Catlin at Pearl Harbor in the fall of 1943. I was an instructor briefly because I made a perfect score on my final examination. This was not because I was intelligent. It was simply because I was the only guy in the class who knew how to take notes and had some study habits. In typical Navy fashion I learned to operate several radar sets but was told to instruct on several others I had never seen before. The class and I together learned how to turn the sets on. As a result, I didn't last too long as an instructor.

But I had been trained on both surface and air search radars of the types used on destroyers. And there was a position open as radar observer on a destroyer that was preparing to embark on an invasion. The idea was to observe the Combat Information Center in operation during combat to improve the instruction in the radar operators' school. The officers discussed the situation and narrowed the choice down to me and Robertson.

It looked like a good adventure because the observer wouldn't stand all those watches and endure the full routine of the regular crew. He would take a cruise and watch other people work.

I was a shy kid who got tongue-tied talking to officers. Robertson wasn't. He was smooth. He outlined his idea of the duty and how he would work it into the school's curriculum. It was the perfect sales pitch. I didn't have a chance. I was disappointed and jealous. Robertson was going to see the war while I stayed there and tried to figure out how to start up stupid radar sets.

We had almost forgotten Robertson when word came that he was dead. The ship ran aground under Japanese shore batteries and was badly battered. Many of the crew were either dead or wounded. It had received a direct hit in the Combat Information Center, killing all of the radar operators and most of the officers.

That was more than forty-one years ago, when a young extrovert sold himself and the bashful kid lost out in an unintentional decision between life and death.

I seldom think about such things. But today, for a brief instant, the memory of a golden youth I never really knew comes back, because he is dead and I am alive. There is neither guilt nor exultation.

I salute him.

(May 27, 1985)

Resolution

U.S. Navy Photograph

U.S. Navy sailors perform a burial at sea wirh full military honors, including the Rising Sun flag, for a Japanese pilot killed in the 1942 Battle of Midway.

The Battle of Midway, fought June 4 through June 7, 1942, is hailed as the turning point of World War II in the Pacific. Leading up to the battle, the island was bombed and strafed by Japanese high level and dive bombers, causing heavy damage. PT Boat Squadron 1, which had traveled 1,385 miles from Pearl Harbor after the attack there, opened fire on the dive bombers and Zero fighters, shooting down at least one of them. Several crewmen aboard PT 25 were wounded.

The attacks were brief, and the boats rescued several downed Marine pilots from the lagoon. Crewmen helped battle fires in hangars and barracks on the island. On June 6, PTs put to sea carrying the flag-draped coffins of eleven Marines who had been killed in the air raids the day before. Burials at Midway were conducted at sea because of the unstable condition of the sand.

Four days later, on June 10, a unique military ceremony was performed for four Japanese pilots who had been shot down. The bodies were shrouded with the Rising Sun flag of Japan. Marine guards fired the same rifle salute as they had accorded their dead comrades. Flags were at half-mast, and services were read by a chaplain before two PT Boats sent the bodies to the deep. At a time when the American people were filled with bitter hatred, this was a moment of civility and military courtesy shown to fallen enemies.

Forty-six years later, on May 30, 1988, Japanese and American veterans met to dedicate a monument on Attu Island in the Aleutian chain off Alaska to honor those from both countries who died in the only World War II battle on North American soil.

In 1942 most Americans had never heard of Attu and Kiska, and probably few remember them. It was a small part of the war, costing the lives of 700 American soldiers and 1,500 wounded. But it was a battle of great misery for both sides and resulted in the death of some 2,500 Japanese, who scored a minor victory even in defeat.

Adm. Isoroku Yamamoto ordered the attack June 4, 1942, as a diversionary move at the time his main fleet was engaged at Midway. Japanese bombers attacked American naval installations at Dutch Harbor on Unalaska Island, inflicting heavy damage. The Japanese invasion fleet landed without resistance.

Pioneer American aviator Billy Mitchell had predicted in 1924 that the Japanese would someday invade the Aleutians. Yamamoto had read Mitchell's book and believed that Fleet Adm. Chester Nimitz would send the remnants of the American fleet northward to counter the invasion.

The Japanese admiral also felt a foothold in Alaska would block any American efforts to invade the Japanese home islands from that direction. Because Japanese codes had been broken, Nimitz did not take the bait. The Japanese were surprised and suffered heavy losses at Midway.

On May 11, 1943, the U.S. Army's 7th Division made a landing on Attu Island. Soldiers suffered frostbite and were harassed by snipers hidden in holes in the tundra. Fog, snow, ice, and freezing winds made the invasion one of great hardship. The Americans advanced ridge by ridge over rugged mountainous terrain until the Japanese were trapped in a valley now called Massacre Valley near Chichagof Harbor. The Japanese made a suicidal banzai charge against American lines and were slaughtered. Others blew themselves up with grenades.

In July 35,000 American and Canadian troops invaded Kiska and found no one on the island. Some 5,400 Japanese troops had been spirited away by a Japanese naval force that had sneaked through American Navy patrols under cover of heavy fog.

Hundreds of Americans died on ships sunk by Japanese submarines. The first casualty from my school was lost on a destroyer that went down with all hands off Attu.

But by 1988 the bitterness and hatred were gone, and the two nations jointly honored their dead with prayers that it would never happen again. Americans, British, and Germans have held similar joint memorials at various battle sites. In this country we have joint memorials at Vicksburg and Gettysburg, honoring the memory of the dead on both sides of our Civil War.

Someday perhaps the United States and Mexico could erect a similar memorial for those who died in battles in 1845-46. Palo Alto Battlefield near Brownsville could be a memorial to the dead of both sides and a monument to the peaceful coexistence of the two neighbors. Such a memorial could aim at unifying rather than dividing our two peoples.

On lonely Kiska Island the Japanese and Americans proved it can be done.

(July 2009/May 31, 1988)

The hymn . . .
was a living memorial
to the dead of all wars.

It happens only a very few times in a lifetime, a moment that seems directed by Divine Will, an instant you never forget. For want of a better word, call it a Golden Moment.

My wife and I were treated to such a rarity last Veterans Day. We were passing through San Antonio and decided to visit the graves of her parents there in Fort Sam Houston National Cemetery.

When we arrived late in the afternoon, flags were flying and chairs indicated a sizable ceremony had honored the dead. We had visited the graves many times, but suddenly we could find no recognizable landmarks. We drove around newly paved roads, looking for the graves.

We parked and walked down rows and rows of headstones, checking the dates of death in area after area. We could not find them at all. It was getting late and we still had miles to go. We were getting exasperated and irritable. Finally we drove to the cemetery headquarters to check maps and learned that the graves were on a new road.

We located the graves, noticing that several rows had been reinterred. Most visitors had gone, and the western sky was colored red and gold.

As we stood at the gravesite, the strains of a bagpipe playing "Amazing Grace" broke the silence. A tall man with erect military bearing, wearing a red beret, piped as he stood at attention over a gravestone across the way.

It was a magic moment. The hymn, meant to honor a buddy, was a living memorial to the dead of all wars. We stood transfixed as the stranger completed the song with a salute.

At that moment the faint bugle sound of evening colors wafted in from Fort Sam Houston. We and the bagpiper stood at attention until the notes faded away. We had tears in our eyes.

The moment was as golden as the sunset.

(November 12, 2000)

Glossary

AA	Anti-aircraft guns
AM	Minesweeper
B-17	"Flying Fortress" a four-engine heavy bomber, used extensively in USAAF raids in Europe
B-24	"Liberator," a four-engine bomber used by U.S. and Allied forces in Europe, the Mediterranean, and the Pacific Theater
B-25	"Mitchell," a twin-engined medium bomber used by many Allied air forces, in every theater of World War II
B-29	"Superfortress," a four-engine, heavy bomber developed after the B-17 and used extensively in air raids over Japan, including the atomic bomb raids on Hiroshima and Nagasaki
BB	Battleship
CA	Heavy Cruiser
CL	Light Cruiser
Corsair	Carrier-capable fighter aircraft that saw service primarily in World War II and the Korean War.
C. Q.	Charge of Quarters
CV	Aircraft carrier
DD	Destroyer
DE	Destroyer Escort
E-Boat	German torpedo boat
F-Lighter	German armored barge
FFG	Guided Missile Frigate
Gedunk	Navy slang for ice cream and other confections
LST	Landing Ship Tank, a vessel created to support amphibious operations
MP	Military Police
MTB	Motor Torpedo Boat, also known as PT—Patrol Torpedo Boat
NRA	National Recovery Administration, a New Deal agency created by President Franklin D. Roosevelt, later declared unconstitutional
NYA	National Youth Administration, the last of Roosevelt's New Deal programs
P-38	"Lightning," a U.S. fighter plane, distinguished by twin tail booms
P-47	"Thunderbolt," one of the main USAAF fighter planes of World War II, effective in air combat but especially adept at ground attack
P-51	"Mustang," a long-range single-seat fighter aircraft
PBY	"Catalina" flying boat, used in anti-submarine warfare, patrol bombing, convoy escorts, search and rescue missions, and cargo transport
PWA	Public Works Administration, a New Deal agency that allowed millions of dollars to be spent on construction of public works
Picket	A small body of troops or a single soldier (or ship) sent out to watch for the enemy
Rate	Standing of a Navy enlisted sailor within the chain of command (Compare to rank for officers.)
Rating	An enlisted sailor's area of specialization
R-Boat	German torpedo boat
Ron	PT Boat squadron, to distinguish from air squadron
SP	Shore patrolman (Navy police officer)
Spad	A World War I biplane fighter aircraft
SBD	"Dauntless," a World War II Navy dive bomber
USAAF	U.S. Army Air Forces
USS	U.S. Navy vessel
Very	Very pistol, used for firing signal flares
VMR	Marine Transport Squadron
Zero	Mitsubishi A6M, a single-seat Japanese World War II monoplane fighter

Index

Symbols

"4F Squadron" 180
8th Air Force 133, 139
10th Field Hospital 109
23rd Infantry Regiment 119
24th General Hospital 115
36th Division 111, 142
41st Armored Division 129
42nd Division 127
45th Division 111, 112
56th Cavalry Brigade 109
82nd Airborne Division 107
86th Torpedo Bomber Squadron 101
101st Airborne Division 7–8, 9
180th Infantry 111
232nd Infantry 127
262 Messerschmitt 143
381st Bomb Group 133
384th Bomb Group 137

A

Aguiar, Bill 137
Alaniz, David J. 131–132
Aleutian Islands 180, 220–221
AM-120 116
Amelia Earhart, the myth and the reality 85
American-Japanese soldiers 41
Andrews Sisters 210
Antwerp, Belgium 7
Anzio 108, 111, 115
Arizona (BB-39) 39, 44, 46, 49, 51
Armistice Day 31–32
Army Signal Corps 35
Astoria (CA-34) 45
Atomic bomb 147–150, 215
Attu 220, 221
Augusta (CA-34) 117
Auschwitz 112
Australia 59, 71

B

Badger (DD-126) 99
Baker, Jackson E. 19–20
Barnard, Dr. James L. 90–91
Barnard, Lynn 91
Barnes, Capt. S.M. 116
Barry, Lt. Cmdr. Dave 97
Bastogne, Belgium 7, 8
Bataan 56, 62, 66
Bataan Death March 54, 62–64, 67, 68
Battles (See specific name.)
Battleship Row 38, 39, 52
Baxter, Col. W. C. 117
Beardsley, Russell 49–50, 177–178
Bednorz, Pat 94–95
Bellheim, Germany 141
Bieghtler, Gen. (Robert) 93
Birmingham, Albert 33
Birmingham, Pvt. Benjamin 33–34
Blu, Bob 102
Blue (DD-387) 49
Boatman, Harvey 58–61
Borie (DD 215) 103–104
Bougainville, Battle of 47
Bradley, Gen. Omar N. 114
Brant, Lt. Cmdr. George E. 103
Bremen, Germany 134
Bridge on the River Kwai, The 58
Buchenwald 137
Bulge, Battle of the 7–8, 108, 125–130
Bulkeley, Capt. Robert J. Jr. 77
Bushchang, 1st Lt. Heinz 129
Bush, George H. W. (President) 155–156

C

Camp Catlin 217
Camp O'Donnell 64
Camp Scurry 109
Carlisle, John 167–168
Carr (FFG-52) 79–80
Carr, Paul Henry 79–80
Carter, R. S. 131
Cartwright, Lt. (unk) 94
Cassino, Italy 131
Castillo, Victor 107–108
Catchings, Virgil 53–54
Chichagof Harbor 220
China Coast attacks 99
Churchill, Winston 150
Cimarron (AO-52) 158–159
Clanton, Leonard 99
Clark Field 62
Clark, Lt. Gen. Mark 115
Clark, Peter 105–106
Cloud, Lt. Dwight 94
Coast Guard 167168
Coast Guard Patrol Craft 7201 167–168
Colombia 18
Comer, John 133–136
Confederate Air Force 141
Connolly, Jack 51–52
Copeland, Robert. W. 80
Corpus Christi Naval Air Station 96
Corregidor 56, 63, 69
Coughlin, Father Charles E. 204
Crossen, (Gunner) 75
Curran, Brigadier E. J. 65–66
Cusack, Radioman R. W. 180, 187

D

Dachau 111
D'Aquino, Iva Toguri 210. See also Tokyo Rose.
Day the Red Baron Died, The 27
D-Day 108, 119, 122
Delaney, Jim 94
Denfield, Vice Adm. L. E. 100
Der, Torpedoman John 75
Dinn, Wallace L. Jr. 72–73
Doenitz, Adm. Karl 212
Dorsey, Tommy 210
DuBose, Lt. Ed 117
Dubrinsky, Lt. 94
Durham, Bull 152
Dutch Harbor 220

E

Earhart, Amelia 84–85
Easley, Billie 101–102
Eisenhower, Gen. Dwight D. 111, 212
Elco boats 180
Elissa 179
Emden, Germany 134
Enemy Below, The 104
Eniwetok 152
Enola Gay 147–148
Enterprise (CV-6) 45

Erdman, Capt. Clifford 84
Eskew, Henry 127–128
Essex (CV-9) 96–97
Essing, Bob 19–20
"Expendables" 169

F

Farmer, Don 89
Firefighting 164–165
Fitzgerald, Carl 196
Fitzgerald, Mr. 196–197
Fitzgerald, Ralph 196–197
Fleet Radar School 217
Flores, Frank 119–120
Ford, Gerald (President) 155–156, 210
Forgy, Chaplain Howell, Lt. (jg) 39
Formosa attacks 99
Forrestal, Secretary of the Navy James 80
Fort Clayton 22
Fort Sam Houston 35, 36, 222
  National Cemetery 222
Foulois, Lt. Benjamin D. 35
Frank, Waldo 117
French Frigate Shoals 189, 206

G

Gamble, Lt. Lester H. 74
Gavin, Gen. Jim 'Slim' 107
General Belgrano 49
George Clymer Liberty Ship 212
Gestapo 123
Gettysburg 221
Gibbons, Floyd 27
Goering, Hermann 140

Goerner, Fred 85
Golden Gate Bridge 207, 212
Gollihar, Ed 18
Golzman, Dan 143
Golzman, Leo 143
Greene, Lt. (jg) James Brent 74
Grey Geese Flyer, The 94
Grizzle, Sgt. 119
Guadalcanal 15, 39, 41, 47, 74, 79, 169
Guadalcanal, Battle of 101
Guam 47, 101
Gus (See Rossberg)
Gutierrez, Simon 41
Guy, Bill 91

H

Hagerty, Ray 174, 186
Hall, J. P. 202
Hansard 202
Hanson, Rear Adm. E. W. 100
Harshbarger, Albert T. 101
Haruna 94
Hatcher, Carl 51
Hatfield (DD 231) 103
Hawaii, "the Big Island" 173
Heaney, Dr. H. Gordon 109
Hershberger, Mrs. Reyna 123–124
Hewitt, Vice Adm. Henry K. 117
Hickam Field 40
Higgins boats 180
Hill, Lon C. III 78, 115–118
Hilo, Hawaii 175–176
Hiroshima, Japan 94, 149, 150, 215
Hirt, Al 137
Hitler, Adolf 146, 212
Hogan's goat 166
Honolulu, Hawaii 36, 52, 194
Honshu 100
Horner, T. Frank 95

Hornet (CV-8) 158
Hourtel, Joe 141–142
Houston (CA 30) 58
Howland Island 84
Huckins boats 180
Hunt, Tom Sr. 137–138
Hunt, William 138
Hutchins Lt. Charles H. 104

I

IG Farben chemical plant 139
International News Service 210
Italian Fascists 123
Italian Partisans 123
Iwo Jima 88–89, 99

J

Jacob Jones (DD-61) 19
Japanese lieutenant commander 81–82
Jarvis (DD-393) 44–45
Java 58, 71
Jodl, Gen. Alfred 212
John D. Edwards (DD 216) 103
Johnson, Albert 38–39
Johnson, Maj. Richard (Dick) 113–114
Jones, Seaman 2/c 177–178

K

Kamikaze 70
Kamikaze planes 89, 90, 102
Kane, Martin 142
Kaneohe, Hawaii 42-43
Kauai 207
King, General 62
Kingman, Rear Adm. H. F. 100
Kiska 220, 221
Knowles, Cline (Chick) 151–152

Korea 108, 139, 143, 217
Koreans 59
Krause, S-Sgt. Vernon 129–130
Kure Island 102, 192, 206
Kurile Islands 90

L

Lawson, Manny 67–68
Legg, Quartermaster John 75
Leverkussen, Germany 134
Leyte 99
Leyte Gulf, Battle of 79
Lido Road 86
Liebenow, William F. 76–78
Litchfield (DD-336) 52
Lochester 33
Lonesome Lady (B-24) 94
Loya, Joe 62–64
Ludwigshafen, Germany 134, 139
Luftwaffe 133, 134
Lumbari Island 76
Luzon 93, 99

M

MacArthur, Gen. Douglas 53, 169
MacCormick, Willie 55–57
Mack, Connie 19
Mallard, C. W. 42–43
Mansheim, Germany 140
Marcus Island 101
Martin, Col. B. J. 65
Martin, R. A. 147–148
Masonic Home and School 97
Mauldin, Bill 110, 111

225

McAuliffe, Brig. Gen.
  Anthony C. 5,
  7–8, 9, 13
McCaleb, Kenneth
  210–211
McComb, R. L. "Bob"
  17
McDonel, Chief Thomas Lee 46–48
Mediterranean 116,
  117
Meico Queen 83
Memorial Day 15–16,
  198
Merrill, Brig. Gen.
  Frank 87
Merrill's Marauders 86
Mexico 221
Midway, Battle of 219
Midway Island 43,
  153, 180–181,
  184–185, 195, 206
Mili Atoll 83
Miller, Don 141
Miller, Glenn 210
Mitchell, Gen. "Billy"
  36–37, 220
Mitscher, Vice Adm.
  M. A. 98
Molokai Channel 180
Monterrey, Mexico 19
Montgomery, Lt. Cmdr.
  Alan R. 74
Moonlight Maid (B-24)
  94
Moosburg, Germany
  131–132, 146
Morris, Rear Adm.
  David R. 96
Mussolini, Benito 124,
  211

N

Nagasaki, Japan 149,
  150, 215
Nale, (Gunner) Leon
  75
Nanking, China 105
Nansei Shota attack 99

National Memorial
  Cemetery of the
  Pacific 15
Nevada (BB-36) 47
New Georgia Island 76
New Orleans (CA-32) 38
Niihau Island 207
Nijegen, Holland 108
Nikoloric, Lt. (jg)
  Leonard A. (Nick)
  74–75
Nimitz, Chester W.
  Jr. 70
Nimitz, Fleet Adm.
  Chester W. 70,
  99, 170
Noonan, Fred 84
Normandy 119, 121
  See also D-Day.
North Africa 107, 109,
  110, 131
North Atlantic 121
Nugent, Lt. Hal 116
Nuremburg, Germany
  146

O

Oahu 173
O'Brien, Joe 155–156
Oglala (CM-4) 44, 45
Okinawa 90, 92, 100
Oklahoma (BB-34) 39,
  47, 49, 51
Omaha Beach 119, 122
Osaka, Japan 149

P

Page, Leland "Boomer"
  117
Palo Alto Battlefield
  221
Panama 17–18
Panama Canal 21–22
Parsons, Jack 51–52
Patch, Gen. (Alexander) 132
Patman, Wright 121
Patrol Torpedo Boats
  74 (See PT.)
Patton 113

Patton, Gen. George S.
  8, 111–114, 146
Paul Jones (DD-10) 17
Pearl and Hermes Reef
  206
Pearl City Yacht Club
  187
Pearl Harbor 38–52,
  153, 169, 170,
  215, 219
Pearl Harbor Survivors
  Association
  51–52
Pelligrino, Matt 18
Pennine, Al 125–126
Pennsylvania (BB-38)
  44
Pershing, Gen. "Black
  Jack" 20
Petroski 193
Pfeifer, Virgil 111–112
Philippine Campaign
  41
Philippine Insurrection
  166
Philippine Islands 53
Philippine Sea, Battle
  of the 101
Phoenix (CL-46)
  49–50
Phoenix (SSN-702) 50
Pineapple juice
  200–201
Poquerolle Island
  117–118
"Praise the Lord and
  Pass the Ammunition!" 39
Prisoners of War
  53–68, 127–128,
  130, 131–132,
  139–140,
  144–146
PT 25 219
PT 37 75
PT 109 76–78
PT 157 76
PT 164 76
PT 210 116
PT 213 117
PT 233 115
PT 256 186

PT 259 153, 169–170,
  182–188,
  208–209
PT 260 214
PT Boats 74, 115–118
  (See also PT Boat
  by number.)
PT Ron 1 219
PT Ron 15 116
PT Ron 26 (See also
  PT 259) 169,
  180, 208
Punchbowl National
  Cemetery, 15
Putnam, G. P. Jr. 84
Pyle, Ernie 111

Q

Quincy (CA-39) 45

R

Ramsey, Charles 44
Rangewell Airdrome
  135
Red Baron, The (See
  Richthofen, Manfred von)
*Red Knight of Germany,
  The* 27
Reeve, Sam 141
Regaine, Ferdinand
  137–138
Reid, Lt. Kenneth 193,
  208
Remmert, Bill 97
Rendova 47
Rhine River 127, 130
Richthofen, Manfred
  von 27
Ridgeway, Gen. Matthew 107
Rising Sun flag 220
Roberts, John D. 141
Robertson, Radarman
  217–218
Roberts, Samuel B. 79
Robinson, Lt. Hugh
  M. 74
Roosevelt, President
  Franklin Delano
  21, 80, 204–205

Roosevelt, President Theodore 19
Roper, Capt. J. W. 100
Ross 215–216
Roswell Military Institute 109
Rota 101
Royal Hawaiian Hotel 194
Russian Army 145
Russians 212
Ryan, A. G. 121

S

Sagan Prison 131
Saipan 165
Samuel B. Roberts (DE-413) 79
San Francisco (CA-38) 39
San Juan Hill 19
Sasser, Sam 84
Schofield Barracks 40, 41
Search for Amelia Earhart, The 85
Searles, Lt. John Malcom 74
Searles, Lt. Robert L. 74
Seifert, Mrs. Lucille. (See Carr, Paul Henry.)
Shannon, Claud 18
Shaw (DD-373) 39, 49
Shenandoah 36
Shook, Winston "Wink" 88–89
Sicily 107, 110, 131
Siegfried Line 130
Simpson, Sgt. 119
"Slot, the" 74
Smith, Jesse 51–52
Smith, Gerald L. K. 204
Smith, John Lee 31
Smith, Lt. Gen. Walter B. 212

Smith, Mrs. Alfred C. 34
Smith, Pfc. Claude J. 25–26
Snyder, Kalmar 214
Solomon Islands 47 (See also Guadalcanal.)
Some Survived. An Epic Account of Japanese Captivity During World War II 67
Southern France 110, 111
Spanish-American War 19
Sprague, Rear Adm. Clifton A. 79
Stalag 1 140
Stalag A-7 131
Stalag 13-C 128
Stalag Luft 3 144
Stanford, Mrs. Ed (Ella) 25–26
Stars and Stripes 111
Steele, P. 23–24
Stilwell, Gen. "Vinegar Joe" 86–87
Stone, Commodore E. E. 100
Stone, Dr. Belo 27–28
Strippel, Dick 85
Sturgeon (SS 187) 69
Submarines 69, 70, 194
Sweinfurt, Germany 134
Switzerland 140

T

Taloa (B-24) 94
Tarawa 173
Task Force 95 151
Taylor, Gen. Maxwell 8
Taylor, Lt. Henry S. 74
Tennessee (BB-43) 47, 51
The Longest Day 107

Thornton (DD 270) 51
Thorpe, E. D. 86–87
Tibbets, Col. Paul Jr. 147
Tiger tanks 129
Tinian 101, 147
Titter, Dale 27
Tojo, Hideki 211
Tokyo, Japan 149
Tokyo carrier attacks 99
Tokyo Rose 210–211
Toulon, France 117
Townsend, Dr. Francis E. 204
Trippe (DD-403) 117
Truax, Ens. Myron Melton 96–98
Truax Field 96
Truax, Frank 98
Truax, Virginia 96, 98
Truman, President Harry S 19, 100, 149, 205
T Square 27 (B-29) 88
Tucker, George 118
Turek, Lt. 94

U

U-Boat 405 104
Ullom, Harry 139–140
Ulrich, Phil 93
Unalaska Island 220
Utah Beach 122

V

V-E Day 31, 212–213, 215
Vela, Fidel 64
Veterans Day 32
Vicksburg 221
Vietnam 139, 217
Vietnam War 108
Villa, Pancho 19
Vincennes (CA-44) 45
V-J Day 31, 215–216

W

Wainwright, Gen. Jonathan 56
Wake Island 101
Walraven, O. D. Jr. 133
Wasp (CV-18) 101–102
Watson, Lt. Warren 7–8
Watson, Lt. Col. Stuart S. 135
Weldon, King 145
West Virginia (BB-48) 47, 51
Whitehead, Carlos 141
William D. Porter (DD-579) 90–91
Williams, "Big Willie" 171–172
Williams, James R. Jr. "Little Willie" 174, 186
Wilmot, Dave 137
Wilson, President Woodrow 31
Winged Defense 36
Wisconsin (BB-64) 99
World War I 23–34, 139
World War II Memorial 2
Worsham, Tommy 144–146
Wright, Joe 83–85
Wright, Rear Adm. W. L. "Bull" 69–71
Wright, Robert 101
Wyatt, Oscar Sherman Jr. 92

Y

Yamamoto, Adm. Isoroku 220
Yeager, Abe 35–37
Yokohama, Japan 149
Young, Gail B. (Spider) 102

www.ingramcontent.com/pod-product-compliance
Lightning Source LLC
Chambersburg PA
CBHW062206080426
42734CB00010B/1807